THE RESILIENT *Educator*

Empowering Teachers to Overcome
Burnout and Redefine Success

Jaclyn Reuter

River Valley Publishing

EST 2020

Published by River Valley Publishing, LLC:
www.rivervalleypublishing.com

Publisher's Cataloging-in-Publication Data
Reuter, Jaclyn, 1989-
    The resilient educator: Empowering teachers to overcome burnout and redefine success / Jaclyn Reuter
       ISBN 978-1-7352409-1-6 (pbk.) | ISBN 978-1-7352409-2-3 (hardcover) |
       ISBN 978-1-7352409-3-0 (audiobook) | ISBN 978-1-7352409-0-9 (ebook)
       1. Teachers—Reflective Teaching. 2. Teachers—Job Satisfaction. I. Title.

LB1775.2 .R48 .R37 2020
371 R317 2020   2020912192

Edited by Rachel Garber
Author Photos by Kayla Taralson.
Cover Design by 100Covers.com
Interior Design by FormattedBooks.com

Printed in the United States of America.

Download Your Free Resilient Educator Reflection Journal!

RESILIENT EDUCATOR
REFLECTION JOURNAL

The Resilient Educator Reflection Journal is a companion to this book. It is designed to help you reflect upon your own practice, goals, and experience as you read.

Download the Resilient Educator Reflection Journal here:

https://bit.ly/resilient-educator-journal-download

CONTENTS

DEDICATION

I would like to dedicate this book to the following people.

My husband, Lucas.
You have brought joy to my life from day one. I'm so grateful to have such a loving, fun, and supportive partner in my life. You are my cheerleader, my sounding board, and my safe place. Thanks for being you.

My daughters, Nora and Alice.
You two make me so proud, every single day. Thanks for helping Mommy achieve her dream. Now it's your turn. Dream big, little ones. I'll be right here to help.

My parents and teachers, past, present, and future.
I have reached this point because of you. I'm called to this vocation because of the example you set for me. You have helped me reach for my potential, and have inspired me to do the same for my children and my students.

INTRODUCTION

When we all chose to pursue a career in education, we knew it wouldn't be a walk in the park. We knew we were choosing a job that would come with extra hours and no extra pay. We were told this vocation was not for those who wanted a "normal" job. What we didn't know was just how hard it could be.

Somewhere down the line, a mentor teacher or a family member who is an educator may have shined some light on the realities of teaching today, but if you are anything like me, your young, idealistic self probably thought you were going to be different. Those things weren't going to happen to you. You were going to change the world, one classroom of students at a time.

These idealistic, and frankly naïve, versions of ourselves dreamed big dreams, poured our hearts and souls into our classrooms, our curriculum, and making our students feel loved and appreciated. We gave and gave until it became clear that something had to go. For many of us, that meant more hours with family sacrificed for the good of our students. It meant less time to dedicate to friends and hobbies and oftentimes, neglecting our own well-being. We pushed ourselves to show up every day for those kids, because they needed us.

If you are like me, you started to burn out. It probably happened a little bit at a time. You may have started struggling to get up in the morning or falling asleep at night. Maybe you started bringing even more pent up stress home. Maybe you stopped taking care of yourself in other ways. Whatever the case was for you, you may not have even noticed what was happening until you felt completely burnt out.

The process of teacher burnout looks different for a lot of us. For many teachers, it can be a slow process taking several months or school years. For some, it can hit you like a punch to the stomach on a random Tuesday. However it happens, teacher burnout can end our love for what we do. This problem affects so many of us, and believe me, bouncing back from this on your own can seem extremely daunting.

That's why I wrote this book. I wrote it for you: the amazing teacher who thinks they can't do this anymore. You, the undervalued educator who has the potential to change the lives of hundreds or maybe even thousands more students before your time in the classroom is over. You, the teacher reading this who is afraid they aren't effective in their job anymore. You, the selfless, loving, teacher who chose this career knowing full-well that this job was going to be one of the toughest things you'd ever do. Despite all of that, here you all are, serving your students the way you do best, but providing them with a chance to learn in a place where they feel safe and valued, every day.

This profession needs you. Your students—past, present, and future—need you. I don't say that to try to guilt you into staying in education. But I think that if you picked up this book, you want to try to make this work. That tells me you're in this for the long haul, and that you may just need some new strategies to help you manage it all.

I have been through the struggle of teacher burnout. I have cried in my classroom, stayed up all night worrying about students, lost my passion for education, and yet, here I am, still teaching. I bounced back from my state of burnout, and you can too. You can put those feelings of negativity away and become an even more encouraging teacher for your students, because now you know what it feels like to want to quit when all hope seems lost. You can come back from this more energized and motivated than ever before. You will be able to empathize with your students in a new way because you know what it means to feel like you've failed and then come back even stronger. You can come out of this period of burnout in your life ready to take it all on again.

If you take nothing else away from this book, I hope you remember this: Going through teacher burnout does not mean you are a bad teacher. It doesn't mean this isn't your calling. It just means you need to take a step back and redefine what being a successful teacher means. It means you need to stop comparing yourself to other teachers who appear to have it all together. You need to be you, the teacher your students love and appreciate, even when they don't show it.

I hope that my story will help all of you rediscover your "why," the reason we all get up and go to school every day when all we want to do is to stay home and sleep; the reason we keep trying to reach that one kid who pushes us away; the reason that we live for the "ah-ha" moments our students have when they finally understand that concept we've been drilling for weeks. It's for that reason that we became and have remained, teachers. I hope that my stories of how I've grown as a teacher and learned to accept the things I cannot change will motivate you to look past the bad and embrace the good. As we all know, teaching is not for the faint of heart. It's for those whose hearts continue to grow Grinch-style every year, leaving enough room for each and every one of the students who walk through the door.

Through telling you my story and reflecting upon what I have learned, I hope to inspire you to keep going, to find value in what you do each day even when you don't feel appreciated, and to notice and celebrate the progress you make toward your success as an educator.

You are an advocate for your students and their abilities to succeed and grow. You are their cheerleader. We all cheer for our students and often forget to cheer for ourselves. So take this time to reflect on the good you do each and every day. Don't forget your "why." If you need a reminder, I hope my stories will spark your memories, and like me, you will bounce back and become ready to take on another year.

PART ONE

Our Purpose

'Far and away the best prize that life offers is the
chance to work hard at work worth doing.'
—THEODORE ROOSEVELT

CHAPTER 1

Finding My "Why"

My first year of teaching was…interesting. I spent many prep periods wondering what the heck I was doing because there was NO WAY that I was good enough for those kids. Or crying over something unkind a kid said to me after refusing to react at the moment. Or stress eating the "prize candy" from my drawer. Or looking for a new job…

While I know that few new teachers have the best year ever during their first year, I felt like I hit rock bottom over and over again. I was a new mom and it killed me to leave my daughter at home. I was pregnant with my second child, financially supporting my family of three on my first-year teacher salary and attempting to make an impact on the approximately 120 students who came through my room each day. I was overtired, overworked, and overwhelmed. On top of it all, I didn't have the group of supportive teacher friends everyone had told me about. I was miserable, and I almost quit.

Here's why I didn't.

There was a student in my class, who I will call Michael, who obviously didn't like me. He was the only student I sent to the office for the entire first semester, and I had some rough kids. Michael was super capable but refused help and adamantly refused to try. I gave him a detention for "noncompliance and disrespect," per the building policy, only to have the consequence overturned by an administrator. You can imagine what came next.

He swaggered back into my classroom the next day with a grin on his face. Not only did the behavior continue (see "no consequence"), but it got worse. Instead of writing an essay I assigned, Michael wrote me a letter that outlined, and I quote, reasons why "nothing you teach me is worth any of my brain space." Wow, right? Ouch. As a first-year teacher, I took this pretty hard. Remember when I mentioned crying in my classroom during my prep periods? Yeah, that was one of those days. I couldn't understand what I had done to earn this kid's total disdain. I was at a loss.

Now, you might be wondering why a kid like Michael would stop me from hanging up the lesson plans and quitting after year one. It turns out, he wasn't just being a jerk because he didn't like me. He was being a jerk because he was in pain. Here's what I learned about Michael:

The day I assigned that essay was the first anniversary of his dad's suicide. At 13, he and his twin brother were left fatherless. Michael was lashing out because he was grieving, and everyone had expected him to "move on." His brother was adjusting well to high school and seemed to be coping with his grief in healthy and productive ways. Well, Michael wasn't ready for healthy and productive. He still needed to be mad, and I was the perfect target for his anger.

After coming to this realization about Michael, my opinion of him totally changed. Suddenly, I was able to allow his sometimes rude and harsh comments to roll right off of me without feeling personally attacked. I was able to see past his anger and see him for the intelligent young man that he is.

Let's flash forward to the end of the school year. Michael is still Michael. He is still my harshest critic, but he started caring about his learning. For our last class novel of the year, we read Ellie Wiesel's Night, a Holocaust memoir. While reading the novel as a class, Michael's outspokenness was FINALLY what I needed. He was the first to gasp and blurt out, "That's disgusting! How could anyone ever think that about another human being?" Cue silence—like "hear a pin drop" silence. His peers didn't know what to say and neither did I. He was the first to process his emotions out loud when something new was described. And when I assigned a reader-response paper at the end of the unit, instead of getting another letter on how I was the worst teacher ever, he actually wrote the paper. He wrote the paper! Michael, the kid who said my assignments were garbage. Michael, who pushed my buttons every day. Michael, the boy who knew grief and could suddenly connect with a text. Needless to say, his essay was amazing. Was it full of grammatical errors and non-academic language? You bet it was; however, it was a beautifully personal view into how he connected losing his dad to the lives of those who also lost their loved ones. I was so proud to be his teacher that day.

While this story is one of many cool stories from that first year, it remains one of my foundational memories from that year. In fact, I kept his angry letter. Yep, the one in which he insulted me and belittled me and my teaching. I keep it to remind myself of one VERY important fact: It's not about me. My student's learning, their reactions to my class, their lives—all of it—is not about me.

I wish my classroom could be a self-contained bubble in which everything else—all of the drama, the family issues, the poverty, and the hurt—could just melt away. But we all know it doesn't work that way. Students come into our classrooms with pain that we may never know about or understand. And we shouldn't just pretend it isn't there. Kids (and teachers) need some grace sometimes. I keep Michael's letter to remind me to give my students (and sometimes, even my colleagues) some grace, even when they don't deserve it.

That next year, Michael was the reason I came back.

I don't know about you, but I was bitten by the teacher bug as a little girl. My parents are both teachers. School and educational issues have been the topic of discussion at the dinner table for as long as I can remember. Even during my "rebellious" college years, during which I rejected the idea of becoming a teacher, I knew that I would eventually end up in a classroom. Education is in my blood.

There was a time when I thought I'd find something else, another calling that would be my ticket out of teaching. That was also the time when I felt burnout coming on strong. Like *really* strong. I'm ashamed to say that some days, I sat in the parking lot, trying to build myself up enough to walk in the door. I was at a point where I hid during prep periods so I didn't have to tell people how my day was. I avoided the staff lounge like the plague and never attended a staff social event. I was a hermit, keeping everyone at a distance just in case I didn't come back next year.

I looked at jobs in nonprofits, bookstores, and in higher education. I applied for jobs I wasn't even close to qualified for. I considered work-from-home gigs, direct sales companies, and starting an at-home daycare so I could be home with my own children. But I kept coming back to teaching. The good parts of my job crept back into my head during my hours of pouring through Indeed.com searches for what else was out there. Suddenly, the thought of going a school year without a classroom full of students just wasn't something I could live with. So I decided to give it another year. And then another. Do I still look at job postings and consider my options? Yep. Do I still struggle to bond with the "lifer" teachers? You bet I do. But those things don't make me a bad teacher, and if you do those things too or have other ways to "keep your options open," that's ok. That doesn't make you a bad teacher. It makes you human. And people like us with real, big, wild feelings can make wonderful teachers.

Sure, I still feel burned out sometimes. I think we all do. But there is something about those lightbulb moments for our struggling students. That feeling of accomplishment that comes from helping your "project" students achieve things they didn't think were possible. Those moments make the late-night lesson plans, last-minute scrambling, and the never-ending piles of grading worth it. Those moments of joy are my "why," my reason I keep going even when it seems like nothing I do is making a difference.

What's your "why?" What's the driving force that keeps you going when you are getting cross-eyed from all of the grading, the coffee is all gone, and you're scrambling late at night for tomorrow's lesson materials on Teachers Pay Teachers (yes, I've been there, too!)?

This spark, this "why" is what can help jumpstart our process of bouncing back. When we remember why we are doing these tough things, it can be like a boost of adrenaline that helps us to continue on. When I set any type of goal for myself, I first visualize the finish line. I imagine this end goal as if it has already happened. Then, whenever I find myself slacking or wanting to quit, I picture the finish line again, and that motivates me to keep going.

When I was trying to get back in shape in order to keep up with my busy children, I took a dance fitness class taught by a teacher friend of mine. She thought I should consider getting certified to teach the class, but I didn't think I could do it. I didn't think I could even take the class, let alone teach it. In the beginning, I was terrible. I've always loved to dance, and I have a decent sense of rhythm, but I had zero endurance. I was in the worst shape I'd ever been in. After the first day, when I had found excuses to leave class to go to the bathroom or fill my water bottle to hide how out of shape I was, I thought to myself, *What if I'm not even in good enough shape to take this class? How could she possibly think I could teach it?*

I talked to my friend about it, and she pushed me to take the training. I knew I had a long road ahead of me before I got to that point, so I made teaching this class the finish line and came up with a road map to get myself there. I started small, challenging myself to do half a class without stopping, then 45 minutes. Finally, I pushed myself to complete the entire class without taking a break. At that point, I felt ready to take the training.

As we all know, teaching a class takes *way* more energy than attending one. Teachers of all kinds pour all of their energy into the lessons they teach, and fitness instructors are no exception. I knew I had my work cut out for me, and I still had a long way to go before I was ready. I practiced getting through a class at the instructor-level, which was a serious challenge for me. Eventually, I got there, and I started teaching my own classes twice a week. I followed my road map, focusing on the "why" behind all of the hours of practicing, learning routines, and building my endurance.

I then applied this experience to my teaching at school. My finish line became making teaching my true vocation, my life's work. From there, I came up with benchmarks: finish my master's degree, present at conferences in my region, celebrate my 30th birthday with my students, and so on. With the end in mind, I continue to add to my road map, a few steps at a time, so that I'm always moving forward. I celebrate the milestones along the way and constantly reflect on my own practice to make things simpler down the road. No matter which benchmark is my focus at the time, I'm always striving to achieve my goal of becoming a "lifer" teacher, like those who have mentored me over the years.

Mini-confession time: I, like my children and students, am motivated by little extrinsic rewards. I sometimes need to reward myself for working towards my goal in order to keep going. I know, it's not the most mature way to handle things, but it works for me. I always find it helps to celebrate my benchmarks once I achieve them. Maybe I'll order a sub sandwich for lunch instead of eating in the cafeteria. Maybe I'll leave my teacher bag at school for a few days and binge watch a TV show with my husband instead of working more at home. Or perhaps I'll dedicate some afterschool time to writing, my favorite hobby, to help myself feel more centered. Whatever you decide to use to reward yourself, decide it ahead of time and then you have mini-goals to strive towards. Or maybe you're more intrinsically motivated than me, and you won't need mini-rewards, but I find the prospect of something just for me in my busy life as a mother, teacher, and wife can be just the thing to keep me motivated when things get tough.

Now it's your turn. What's your "why?" What's your finish line? Do you want to teach until retirement? Do you want to teach until you have kids and then stay home? Do you dream of becoming an administrator some day? Whatever your goal is, write it down, either here in this book, in a notebook, or in the free printable Resilient Teacher Reflection Journal (See the front of the book for the link!). Then come up with some benchmarks that will help you get there. From there, you can continue your journey away from burnout and towards your goals.

Commit yourself to this road map, picture the end goal, remember your "why," and don't give up! Let your goal drive you when nothing else is working. I speak from experience when I say, you can do this.

Pause for Reflection:

Write down your end goal here. What's your "why?"

Now, what benchmarks can you use to get there? What steps will be necessary for you to attain your goal?

CHAPTER 2

Personal Success

When my youngest daughter was two years old, I was not in a good place. I felt awful, all of the time. I was unhappy at work, unhappy at home, and unhappy in my skin. Regardless of how I felt, I pasted on fake smiles, and many people who were close to me at the time had no idea I was hurting. I thought that if I let it show how unhappy I was, then I would truly be failing. So I kept putting on that mask, day after day.

Thinking back on that time in my life can be painful because I've come so far from that miserable version of myself. But I think it's important to reflect upon that period because seeing how far I've come gives me a boost of self-confidence. I think, "If I can get through that in one piece, I can get through this other trying time in life." It helps give me perspective when I am feeling down on myself.

I still remember the point when it all changed for me. It wasn't anything someone else did for me or even a huge revelation by any means. I hit my tipping point, and from then on, there was no turning back.

While playing outside with my daughters, my little one wanted me to climb on the playground with her. She wasn't quite confident enough to do it all by herself. So I climbed up there and we laughed and played pirates with my oldest, looking through the telescope at the grass around us. Then, it was time to ride the slide back down. I was going to climb down and then catch my little one at the bottom, but she wanted to sit in my lap on the slide. So, I tried. Unfortunately for me, (and for her), it didn't go so well. I tried to climb into the slide, but I didn't fit. I was mortified. In order to save face with my daughters, I held my little one and sort of side-ways slid down the slide.

This moment of embarrassment, while really not a big deal in the grand scheme of things, made me take a closer look at what I was doing with my life. Isn't it odd, *the things that light a fire under us? In my mind's eye, I saw myself half sliding, half pushing myself down that slide as a ridiculous metaphor for how I was living my life. I was pushing myself through my life, and not truly living it. I started to reexamine why I was so unhappy, and why I wasn't doing anything about it. From that point on, I decided I was done with forcing myself through life. I wanted to start living it. Today, I can proudly say that I am no longer coasting through life. I am finding success and joy in the little things.*

We all know that feeling successful can help us move through life without getting in our own way. When we don't feel successful, the feelings of self-doubt and inadequacies many of us experience can become huge roadblocks for us, making it nearly impossible to keep moving forward towards our goals. So what would it take for all of us to feel successful?

According to the Merriam-Webster dictionary, success can be defined as a "favorable or desired outcome." While this definition leaves a ton of wiggle room for interpretation, many of us look for more than just a "favorable" outcome when we look to our own success.

For me, my definition of success was pretty much all-encompassing. I expected a lot of myself during my first few years of teaching. Here was my to-do list (copied from my old teacher planner):

1. Become a good teacher.
2. Earn my master's degree by the end of year two.
3. Be a good parent.
4. Earn recognition at work.
5. Advise a successful after-school activity.
6. Establish and coach a new high school speech team.
7. Write my YA book.
8. Find and maintain a strong group of teacher friends.
9. Keep my mental health in check.
10. Lose my baby weight in one year.

Ok, so did I go a little over-the-top? Yes. But I saw it as a good thing to have and be working towards (mostly) measurable goals. Was I successful in achieving all of those things? No way.

I think I can safely say I accomplished three things on that list. That percentage wasn't good enough for me. Needless to say, that negatively impacted item #9 on my list. My mental health was not in great shape. I knew I needed to make a change.

So, going into my third year of teaching, I decided to narrow it down a bit. Here was my new list:

1. Be a good mom.
2. Be a good teacher.
3. Find and maintain ONE good friendship.
4. Exercise (see: baby weight).
5. Work on my mental health.

Better, right? This list is half as long, but is it manageable? Maybe. And I did make some good progress on most of those things.

I have come to own a few positive things about myself. First, I am a good parent. I am not a perfect parent, because seriously, who is? But I love my children and make them a priority every day. They know they are loved and supported and will always come first. Second, I still have that best teacher friend who has helped me through the highest and lowest parts of my teacher and mom life. I found a cheesy Facebook post that sums up how our friendship began just perfectly. It is entitled "How an Introvert Makes Friends." It is a pie chart filled in all the way with the caption, "An extrovert finds, likes them, and adopts them." That's pretty much Jenn and me. She was my rock when I got divorced and when I wasn't making my mental health a priority, she gently (ok, maybe not so gently) pushed me to take care of myself. Third, I committed two to three hours per week to exercise, and over the course of one year, I lost enough weight to once again feel comfortable in my skin. Am I as thin as I wanted to be? Nope, but I decided I'd rather be happy than skinny. And finally, I have made my mental health a priority. Writing this book is an example of this. I am dedicating time to writing, which is something that helps me find peace in my crazy busy life. However, I know I still have a long way to go.

Now, I know that many teachers have solid mental health and do not struggle with depression or anxiety. To them, I say, I am so happy for you. Truly, I am. However, I do not fall under that category.

Depression and anxiety take turns driving my metaphorical car when not kept in check. Sometimes, I feel like I'm being dragged behind the car. Other times, I'm simply trapped in the backseat, trying to dictate where we are going next. But lately, I feel like I've taken the wheel. When I make myself a priority, I can shove depression and anxiety into the trunk for a while. And although they are always there in the background, I no longer have to go where they lead. These are my good days.

And that, dear readers, is what I am calling personal success. When reflecting upon that definition of success from the beginning of the chapter, I'd say keeping my mental health in check is a "desirable outcome," so I'm going to take it!

Now, I want you to take a moment for reflection. Think about what personal success means to you. What desirable outcomes are you seeking in your personal life? Next, I want you to consider what might be getting in your way. Just like before, jot your responses down in your book or in your Resilient Teacher Reflection Journal. Remember, there are no wrong answers, and it's ok if you haven't figured out what your next steps are yet. You'll get there. It took me a while too.

Pause for Reflection:

What does personal success look like for you?

What is getting in your way?

What can you do to devote at least an hour this week to eliminating your obstacles and working on this personal goal?

Are you fighting a battle with mental health issues? Are you in a relationship that brings more pain than joy? Are you stuck in a job that leaves too much to be desired? Do you just need some well-deserved "me time?" Whatever battle you're fighting on your journey to personal success, please don't give up. I know that being a teacher can sometimes be all-encompassing and it makes it hard to focus on ourselves, especially if we have family or friends who need us. But please, make a promise to yourself that you will give it a try. A *real* try. Not a 6th grader—I tried for 5 minutes and now I need help—try. (You all know what I mean…)

I was reminded the other day that I can't fill everyone else's cup if I'm running on empty. That was a wakeup call that I really needed. I'm guilty of running on fumes for too long, and not taking time to recharge. That's usually when I feel most burned out. When I see others in need of my time and attention, I put aside my own needs to be what they need at that moment, regardless of the personal consequences. By neglecting my own needs, I can help others for a while, but then, something else always slips. This is what I am trying to avoid. My sometimes hypocritical actions aside, I have learned that while the "self-care" craze can sometimes be a bit over-emphasized, taking care of ourselves is absolutely critical to our success. One more time for the people in the back: without taking positive steps toward taking care of ourselves, we cannot find true personal success.

So how can we take care of ourselves in our crazy busy lives? We'll delve deeper into this topic in the chapter on Self-Care, but I think this issue is so important that it is worthy of more than one mention. For me, it often looks different than it does for my colleagues and friends. Many of them need to go do something such as go to happy hour or get a massage. If that's what works for you, then, by all means, do it! For me, I find that moments of gratitude and focusing on things that have gone well help me to feel successful, and when I feel successful, I have the energy to do things that are good for me.

For example, when I feel like a good teacher after a good day at school, I feel energized to make dinner for my family instead of just throwing in a frozen pizza. If I have a good day, I have the energy to play a game with my kids after homework time instead of putting on Netflix. Then, when I tuck them in at night after reading stories, I can sit for a moment in gratitude for a good day. When I have the motivation to do good things for my family at home, I feel like a good mom and wife. It's a domino effect for me, when

I feel successful at school, I can tackle my favorite job: being a Mom to my daughters. Maybe it should be the other way around, and this domino pattern makes it seem like I prioritize school over my home life, but that couldn't be further from the truth. I simply prioritize making each day as positive as possible so that when my day is over, I can look back on the day with a smile.

It may appear over-simplistic to some of you, but I have always found joy in the little things. I don't need a Teacher of the Year nomination or some other form of recognition to feel successful. I find joy in helping my students enjoy learning. I find joy in helping my children have a good end to each day. This helps me feel successful.

Take a minute now and think about the last time you felt successful as a person. Did you stay after school to help a colleague with a project plan? Did you visit a lonely family member? Did you achieve a personal goal? Whatever it is, focus on that for a moment. Let yourself stay in that mental state for a while and think about how you felt. I know that when I'm able to do something extra for a student or find success after teaching a well-planned lesson, I feel a boost of energy. It makes it easier to have good teacher days.

Now that we have a focal point for our new definitions of personal success, let's carry that with us as we make new to-do lists for ourselves. If making time for a friend after a crazy week makes you feel personal success, call them! If playing a game with your kids instead of encouraging them to go outside to play with friends makes you feel like a successful parent, play on! If doing a yoga workout in your living room makes you feel strong and centered, Namaste!

Put things on your personal to-do list that bring you joy, even if they are little things. If you feel like a successful and happy person, you can fill your own metaphorical cup, and in turn, you can then fill the cups of the other people in your life. Make feeling like a successful person a priority, and you'll be amazed how that energy will follow you into the other areas of your life, including your life as a teacher.

Pause for Reflection:

When was the last time you felt successful? What did you take away from this experience that can be carried forward into future decisions?

Personal Success To-Do List: What are three things you could accomplish this month that would make you feel successful?

    1.

    2.

    3.

CHAPTER 3

Professional Success

A handwritten note can go a LONG way towards lifting a person's spirits. I know that when my students take time to write a little note or when a colleague puts a "bucket filler" note in my mailbox, it really makes my day. One of the paraprofessionals at my last school was the best at this. She made it a priority to let other people know that they were important to her. She is one of the rare gems that can really make a tough day seem a little better. I still have some of her bucket filler notes in my drawer. What a difference a little note can make.

That same year, one of my students gave me a card for teacher appreciation week. It is one of those things that comes with me from classroom to classroom. I kept it for those rainy days when I needed to lift my spirits. What she wrote helps me feel like I succeeded that year. While I know that this student wrote cards for each of the five teachers on our team, it didn't make her words any less impactful. My favorite line is "I love how when I come into your classroom, I know I am safe."

Wow. Talk about a tear-jerker, right? I always strive to create a safe and welcoming atmosphere in my classroom, but to hear that from a student was a "wow" moment for me. I thought, "Yes, this is why I'm here." Whether or not she remembers a thing we studied, I hope she remembers that my classroom was, is, and will always remain, a safe place for her, just as it is for all of my students.

Remember that to-do list I had for myself? Well on both my original and my new-and-improved lists, I wrote, "be a good teacher." First of all, "good" is extremely vague. How in the world do you quantify this? Some people (not teachers) look to test scores. Some look to evaluations done by our administrators. But I don't think either of these is an accurate measure of a teacher's ability. A "good" teacher is many things, none of them dependent upon test scores or one-time snapshots of a lesson. A good teacher is someone who does what's best for kids, not what's best for them. A good teacher is someone willing to adapt and change to meet the needs of their students. A good teacher cares. A good teacher sees students as kids first, and learners second. While this is probably not new information to you, I know that for some of us, it's easy to look at the teacher next door and think, "Wow, they're awesome," but it's sometimes much more difficult to look in the mirror and say, "I am awesome."

I know that is SUPER cheesy, but it's true. I can just about guarantee if you are a teacher who cares enough to read a book about how to stick it out when it would be much easier to quit, someone thinks you are an awesome teacher. You may never be nominated for Teacher of the Year. You may be turned down for an administrative role. You may have all of your ideas rejected at curriculum writing meetings, but I promise you, there is a kid somewhere who left your class a changed person.

Let's define professional success for teachers. We already established that test scores and evaluations are not the "be all, end all" for measuring our competence. So what does being a successful teacher mean to you?

Before I answer that question myself, I have another story for you:

I had a student, who I will call Laura, who was a struggling English student. She scored below grade level on standardized tests and her previous grades were not super impressive. It's weird, I know, but I remember that she earned D's (and sometimes lower than that on tests) in my class at the beginning of the year. By the end, she was earning B's. She was over-the-moon excited and proud of herself. We celebrated together each time her work got better, and she was truly committed to getting better. Laura left my class a stronger English student than she had been when she started, and I was so proud to be her teacher.

A few years later, I was working at another school in town. I walked down to the auditorium on my prep to see the crowd of music students there for a regional band contest (reminiscing a bit about my high school band and choir days) and I felt arms go around me from behind.

Now all of you elementary teachers probably don't think it's odd getting hugs from students, but it's a rare thing at the high school level. Needless to say, I was a bit taken aback. The kid stops hugging me and I turn around to find Laura! She looked SO grown up (she was a senior) and confident.

We spent a few minutes getting caught up and she told me all about the band piece she was playing for the contest that day. She was such a happy young lady, which warmed my heart. I love seeing former students, especially those who impacted me as Laura did. Before she left, she said this: "Oh, I almost forgot! I wanted you to know that I am taking AP English this year. I have had all As and Bs since I left your class. And it's because of you." Cue goosebumps.

I choked back some tears and we celebrated like we did when she was in my class. I told her how incredibly proud I was of her for never giving up on herself, even when it was tough. She left me beaming and I cried my way back to my classroom, totally stunned.

Laura is a perfect example of how the things we do today can have long-term impacts on our students. To quote a former principal of mine, "We are planting trees, not wheat." This is so true because some of the things we teach and the ways we interact with our students can leave a lasting impact. Our "good teacher" days, the ones when all of our lesson plans go off without a hitch and we see light bulbs go off across the classroom are awesome, but there is something about a former student telling us we helped them believe in themselves that nothing else can top. Laura made me feel like a good teacher that day.

So how do we feel successful when we are up to our eyeballs in grading, and we have to go back and re-teach something our students just aren't grasping, and parent-teacher conferences are just around the corner, and when the teacher down the hall can close the door after his last student and never bring anything home?

Unfortunately, there isn't a one-size-fits-all answer to that question. Here's what I think. I think we need to redefine what it means to be professionally successful.

Professional success is defined by most of society as earning a bunch of money, getting promoted, starting your own business, or something else along those lines.

Pause for Reflection:

How do you define professional success for educators?

As teachers, not all of those things are even in the realm of possibility. So I believe we need our own definition. While I am fully aware that I don't have the perfect answer, I have some ideas that might help.

Step One:

We need to stop (or avoid) taking it personally when our students don't get it. Even the best teacher in the world is not going to get every single kid to learn a concept the first time around. We also can't take it personally when they don't appear to care enough to learn it, either. Because we don't always know what is going on in our student's lives outside of our classrooms. Some of them have more to deal with than anyone their age ever should.

The first year I taught 6th grade, I had a challenging group of students. In their defense, they were dealing with some serious stuff at home. One student in particular really stands out in my memory. This young man was struggling with severe ADHD and his meds, which he relied upon heavily, were given to him sporadically to put it nicely. Sometimes his mom said they couldn't afford them, other times he just didn't take them. He would literally bounce off the walls in the hallway and hurdle over furniture in our team area on the way to his classes. He was disinterested in schoolwork on good days and defiant on the not so good ones. But he was a good kid, and my whole team really liked him. We just couldn't understand why he wouldn't try.

And then one day, his mom went to jail. I won't go into details, but my student and his siblings went into separate foster homes. This was obviously devastating to a young man going through such a foundational time in his life. To make matters worse, his mom didn't want to see the kids and would skip out on visitation appointments. The problems just got worse for this student. He got more defiant and short-tempered. He would wander the school instead of coming to class. This young man was spiraling, as he felt a severe lack of control in his life.

Fast forward to a few weeks later to when we did a blackout poetry project. I told the students they could create a poem about whatever they wanted. This young man pretended to blow it off, playing the "cool kid," which was par for the course for him. But when I saw his completed poem, tears started rolling down my face. It read: "Tears fill my eyes, as we can go home again." He illustrated it with a single eye, crying tears that covered the bottom of the page. I had never before been so moved by a student's work. All he wanted was his family, home together again.

While it can be so easy to do, we have to stop taking it personally when kids don't get it or when they lash out. Rationally, we all know that these behaviors often stem from a place of pain, but in the moment, we can forget this fact and take student behaviors to heart. We need to let go of these feelings or moving forward in our journey towards professional success will continue to get sidelined.

Step Two:

We need to be ok with other teachers being the "favorites." This one is hard for me. I love my students so much I would literally put myself between them and harm's way. I tell them during our lockdown drills that if someone comes into my classroom looking to hurt my students, they will have to go through me. There is not a doubt in my mind that I would defend each and every one of my students until the end if push came to shove. Yes, even the naughty ones who I blame for my grey hair. But guess what. Most of them like one of their other teachers more than they like me. Some of them are little angels in the classroom next door and then when they are in my classroom, they try my patience, Every. Single. Day. I've come to accept the fact that while not all of my students like me, they know I care about them, and that is good enough.

Nearly every day of the school year, I hear from my students how amazing my colleagues are. I hear how nice they are. I hear about how they hand out candy and prizes and extra credit left and right, and frankly, I can't keep up with that. I didn't get into teaching to be everyone's favorite, but every once in a while, it's nice. And every once in a while, a student will come along with whom I have a truly special connection.

Last year, I met a young man who had obviously been through some significant trauma. I never learned what exactly happened to him, but he proudly boasted to anyone who would listen that he prided himself on how disrespectful he could be to adults. He just enjoyed being rude to teachers and principals and counselors and paraprofessionals and anyone else who tried to help him.

His attitude was clearly a way of keeping us all at arm's length, but I didn't let it keep me away. A former principal of mine told me, "Every kid needs an adult who's crazy about them." That year, I knew nobody else was crazy about this particular kid, so I made it my goal to shower him with support until he let me in. No one was more surprised than me when it worked. He yelled and insulted me and disrespected me in front of the other students the whole way there, but when he finally accepted that I was there to help him, I saw a whole new side of him. I made it my goal to make him smile every day, and when he wouldn't I would tell him I'd continue to embarrass myself until he put me out of my misery. It worked every time. His smirks made my day.

Now, none of that means I was his favorite, and quite frankly I think he just tolerated me because deep down, he's a great kid. Regardless of if I was his favorite, that kid knew my classroom was his safe place. He started coming to me on my prep to work on things he didn't get done. He read the graphic novels I recommended to him, and then made his friends read them. At the end of the year, he proudly introduced me to a group of his friends from another team in our school. That moment made it all worth it. What I do know is I was able to make a difference for that young man. That's worth all of the "Best Teacher" mugs and Teacher of the Year nominations combined to me.

Do all of my students like me? I highly doubt it. I push them and I challenge them and I call them out on their nonsense. But they know I'm there for them. They know my classroom is a safe place. And they know that no matter what they do, I still care.

Step Three:

We need to accept the fact that we may never earn an award or any kind of recognition from our school or district. For people who are "words of affirmation" people, this can be ROUGH. Those whose love languages require affirmation to feel valued and appreciated can really struggle with this. The struggle can be VERY real when you work 50+ hours a week trying to make a difference, only to be passed up for an award at the end of the year. I totally get it, and if you are feeling that way, know that what you are feeling is valid.

But remember, if you care enough about your job to read books to try to avoid burning out and quitting teaching, you are most certainly a good teacher. Bad teachers would not care enough to make it to chapter two of this book. Good teachers look to learn and grow, and that's what you are doing. So, "words of affirmation" people, listen closely:

You have been, are, and will be the teacher of the year in the heart of at least one student to come through your classroom. You are awesome. You are appreciated. Please consider this a small affirmation of all you have, do, and will continue to accomplish as an educator. THANK YOU for being the teacher that you are.

A few years ago, a student of mine applied to attend West Point. If you know anything about the admission process, you know that it can be stressful for even the most ambitious young person. This student was, for lack of a better word, iconic. She wore flouncy, floral dresses and combat boots, wrote poetry, and was the best welder in her Career and Technical Education classes. She even gave me a lesson on welding one day. The project we made together sits on a shelf in my classroom as a constant reminder that my students have so much to teach me.

I was lucky enough to be this young lady's cheerleader at our school. She was smart, hard-working, and exceptionally kind to everyone. All of her teachers and coaches and directors loved her. But when the call came that told her she had been accepted at West Point, she let me share that moment with her. We jumped up and down in the hallway and she cried happy tears as her life trajectory changed in a heartbeat. She no longer felt she had any limits to her dreams. And I was lucky enough to share that joyful moment with her.

I know that doesn't mean I'm the best teacher or coach or anything like that. In fact, I know I'm not. But what that meant to me is that for that special moment for my student, she chose me to share in her nervousness and excitement. That call could have been a rejection. Either way, I would have been there to support her, and I think she knew that. She knew I was a safe person to share that moment with regardless of the outcome. I'll take that over a plaque to hang on my wall any day.

While these steps are not all-encompassing, I know that by focusing on these three ideas, I have found myself coming up with other ways to define professional success. Let's go back to the "we're planting trees, not wheat" idea. Breaking down this metaphor logically, we can come to understand that our students, at whatever age we teach, are still growing. Maybe their trees are more fully-developed, maybe they have already established their belief systems and chosen the path they want to take in life. Perhaps our young ones' trees have barely taken root and they need nurturing and protection from things that will prevent their growth. Or maybe their trees have been ripped out of the ground by the things they deal with in their lives. These transplanted trees often need the most patience and TLC. The shock of being transplanted can slow their growth, and we as teachers need to focus on helping them thrive.

Ok, I'll stop with the tree metaphors, but do you get what I mean? Our students will continue to grow long after they leave our classrooms, so we need to focus on the long game. What skills, values, and knowledge will they take with them when they go?

Pause for Reflection:

What skills, values, and knowledge do you want your students to take with them when they leave your class?

How can you shift your focus to the long game in your classroom?

Let's go back to my story about Laura. She is a great example of the long game. When she was in my class, we focused on her goal of improving just a little bit at a time. Her goals were manageable and measurable, but after she left my class, she kept going. To go from being a D English student to taking an AP course is a huge achievement. Laura showed me what it means to find success in the little things. While it wasn't a little thing for her, having one student out of 120 students share how they accomplished their goals may not always feel like the best success rate, but believe me, it is. I'll take 1 out of 120 if it means that 1 is better off because I was able to help them.

CHAPTER 4

Leaving a Legacy

A few years ago, I picked up the keys to my new classroom in a new school, and surprisingly, there was a piece of mail for me in the office. It was a graduation announcement from a former student. This young man was my student when he was a freshman, and he had moved to another state for his last few years of high school. His letter went something like this: "I don't know if you'll remember me but..."

I'm going to stop right there. Of course, I remembered him. I wish I could say that I remember every one of my students, but, unfortunately, my mind palace isn't as secure as Sherlock's. But this kid, I remember—not because he was a particularly exceptional student—but because I always saw him as an exceptional person. He was an average student who really cared about learning. (I don't know about you, but give me a room full of average-ability kids who care any day.) But what I remember best about this young man was his kindness. He wasn't the most popular kid in the class, but I think you would have been hard-pressed to find someone who didn't like him. He's one of those gentle souls who was content to let others be the loudest, fastest, and most outspoken in the group.

When I opened his card, I was honestly shocked. He wrote that I had made an impact on him and he wanted me to know that he still thought about my class. His note couldn't have come a better time. I was nervous to start at a new school and I was doubting my choice to return to the classroom after two years in an instructional technology role. His note sealed the deal for me. I thought, "Yep, this is where I should be." And here I remain—hopeful to make an impact on my current and future students.

Leaving a legacy looks different for everyone.

For some, leaving a legacy might include a teacher of the year award, a perfectly written curriculum left for future teachers, a former student going on to earn accolades, or even a classroom or program named for them. While all of these things are awesome, and for "words of affirmation" people, some of these things probably sound like something you would appreciate greatly, unfortunately, we all know it doesn't work that way.

So how does it work? How can we as teachers leave a legacy? Is it in the content we teach? Maybe. I still remember what some of my teachers taught me and some of the big projects I completed. Is it the speed at which we grade assignments? Haha, nope! But wouldn't it be nice to get a little gratitude for grading all of those essays in one weekend?

Think back to the best teachers you had as a student. What do you remember about them? What legacy did they leave behind? For me, I clearly remember one-on-one conversations with two teachers: one from middle school, and one from high school. Interestingly, they were both my math teachers.

In middle school, the struggle was very real for me. I was not popular; in fact, I was the opposite. I distinctly remember some of the cruel things my bullies said to me. Needless to say, I didn't do so well socially. Academically, however, I would say I was above average, mostly because I cared about my grades. I was typically a pretty good student, but one of my teachers noticed me not living up to my potential. He pulled me aside and talked to me about it, without talking down to me, without making me feel ashamed, but rather he encouraged me to be better, to work harder, and to not be afraid of being the "smart kid."

This teacher left a legacy with his students by being that sounding board for me and for other students like me. I still see him (he and I teach in the same town) and every time I do, I'm reminded of the lessons he taught me. While I don't remember which formulas I learned to solve or which units I struggled with, I remember the life lessons he taught me about never being satisfied with anything but my best, even when caring about school wasn't the "cool" thing.

In high school, I had a similar experience as a senior in AP Calculus. I had finished my first semester, been accepted into my college of choice, and was ready to start competing for scholarships. Cue the senior slump. Suddenly, I was ok with earning B's on tests and assignments. I was ok with finishing "most" of my homework instead of staying up at night until it was done. I figured, hey, I've already made it into the college I want to attend, and as long as I keep my GPA decently high, I'll be fine.

Enter an awesome teacher: My AP Calculus teacher asked me to stay after school. This was a BIG deal for me because I was a "good kid," and I didn't get in trouble. So when I entered her classroom after school, needless to say, I was nervous. She offered me a Diet Coke and said, "Let's chat." *Gulp.* My brain was running a mile a minute. *What had I done? Did someone accuse me of cheating? Did I fail a test?* Well, it wasn't quite that bad, but *man,* did this teacher have that "mom shame" thing down...

She told me that she was noticing a downward slump this semester and that I was going to be disappointed in myself when the GPA that I had worked SO hard for was gone. After three and a half years of studying, doing any extra credit I could, and generally devoting myself to my education, letting it take a dive in my last year, well, I wouldn't be proud of the end result. Woah. Talk about a guilt trip. I was so embarrassed. Yes, I knew that I had stopped putting in my best work. Yes, I knew I could do better. But for my teacher to take the time to first, notice the change, and second, to try to do something about it was amazing.

I left her room that day partially ashamed of myself, but mostly feeling driven, driven to make her and myself proud. I was so grateful for that chat, and I don't know if she would even remember it, but it was a turning point for me as a student. I have carried that memory with me and have used similar methods on my own students to try to motivate them to work towards success.

So what do these two teachers have in common? You guessed it. They left a lasting legacy with me, their student, without receiving a plaque, without a classroom named after them, and without much obvious gratitude from me.

Looking back, I wish I would have gone out of my way to thank them, but I was a teenager focused on my own issues. Now as a teacher myself, I know what it takes for a teacher to go out of their way for a student in those situations. I know what it takes to pinpoint each students' individual potential and then help them track their progress along the way. I know what it means to spend more time than I already do at school focusing on an individual student when I could be home with my kids.

Both of these teachers could have said, "She made her choice, so she'll have to deal with the consequences." But they didn't. They chose to leave their mark on me even when I know they were just as tired and overworked as I feel somedays.

This is how we leave a legacy. We push past barriers and classroom contests to impart what wisdom we have learned upon our students. We prioritize teaching students to be good people with strong work ethics rather than just good test-takers. By shifting our focus to seeing our students as people rather than just as a faceless group, we get to teach kids that become thinkers instead of just recipients of knowledge, and we can leave a lasting legacy.

What kind of legacy are you leaving behind? Are you the teacher who runs a homework club at lunchtime? Do you find books for your reluctant readers at Barnes and Noble on the weekends? Do you greet each kid with a smile, every day, regardless of how stressed you are? However you are showing up for your students, know that you can truly leave a lasting impact on your students, year after year, even when you think all you are doing is your job. This job that we all have chosen means that for some students in a past, present, or future class, we will leave a legacy that will continue to help motivate them, long after they sit in our classrooms.

So how do we do it? How do we push past the standards and the other crazy expectations on us to truly make an impact on our students? Here are a few of the steps I take to make sure I leave a mark on my students each year:

1. **Set the stage on day one.**

    On the first day of school, I look past all of the craziness that comes with a new school year and really show up for my students. I walk kids to class, I help them memorize locker combinations, I run around like a chicken with my head cut off until every single one of them knows where they need to go. One year, I did 16,000 steps by early afternoon, and I never left my hallway. (I always pick the worst days to wear heels...) This display of hustle for my students sets the tone for all of the other days when they need help. They know from day one that Mrs. Reuter is there to help them. Then, regardless of if they need help with homework or friend drama or a lost calculator, they come back to me time and again because I have established myself as a safe zone.

    This continues once they get into my classroom as well. I stress how their well-being is my top priority and talk about how I see them as individuals and not just as a classroom full of students. I tell them about the times I've gotten help in the past, and that there is no shame in needing a helping hand, whether that's with academics or just life. Either way, I'm there for them.

2. **Celebrate the tangential discussions.**

In my classroom, my sixth graders could earn gold medals for finding the potential for a tangential conversation. Their curious minds jump from one topic to big picture issues at the drop of a hat. During our first week of school this year, we discussed how science, religious studies, and history could coexist in our academic world for AN HOUR when we were supposed to be talking about the Stone Age. Their curiosity was so inspiring that we just had to do it. By the end of the year, my students were still talking about that discussion and how it reshaped their thinking about studying those subjects. Sometimes there are gold mines in those tangential questions that can inspire students to take their learning outside the classroom. By allowing this level of inquiry, I put the students in the driver's seat of their own education and show them that their questions and thoughts have value in my classroom.

3. **Set the bar high, and keep raising it.**

Setting your expectations high and then continuing to raise them creates an environment in which growth is celebrated and coasting is unacceptable. I once had a conversation with a person who believed I expected too much from my students. Now, I have a lot of respect for this person, but I disagreed with them. They thought the type of analysis assignment I gave was above their level. So, I showed them what my students had achieved. They rose to my challenge, stretched themselves, and dug deep into a piece of literature. When we were done, I told those kids that they didn't just raise the bar a little bit, they collectively shoved it up a notch. As the year went on, I kept pushing them to think deeper and to back up their opinions like the scholars they were when they were in my classroom.

Did we get through every unit I had planned? Nope. We did something better; we dug deep into our content and pushed ourselves to grow and learn. I learned right alongside them. By showing our students that we expect a lot from them, we are showing them that we care about more than test scores and essay grades. We show them that their progress matters, that their voice matters, and that their potential is important to us.

As teacher and poet Taylor Mali writes, "I make kids work harder than they ever thought they could. I can make a C+ feel like a Congressional Medal of Honor and an A- feel like a slap in the face." We have the power to impact our students beyond the content we teach. We can create environments in which students crave learning and personal growth in the ways we approach our days in the classroom. Are we still held accountable for standardized tests, common assessments, and required reading lists? Of course, we are, but what we do in between all of those things are what help us leave lasting impacts on the students we teach. It is the collection of all of those little things that help us leave a legacy.

Pause for Reflection:

Think back to your former teachers. What kind of legacy did they leave behind?

What legacy do you wish to leave behind as a teacher?

PART TWO

Our Time

"*The best part about being a teacher is that it matters. The hardest part about being a teacher is that it matters every day.*"
—TODD WHITAKER

CHAPTER 5

Working "Full Time"

*I*nstead of another student story, this time I'm going to tell you one of my stories, and I think it will sound familiar to many of you. Keep in mind, I do not tell this story to depress you or to try to garner any sympathy; however, I tell it to set us up for our topic of time. Here's my story of time as a new teacher.

During my first two years of teaching, I felt like I was barely keeping my head above water. I felt as if I was one off-day away from having a breakdown and quitting. I missed my children, I felt like I wasn't getting anywhere with my students, and I felt like I had ZERO wiggle room in my day. Here's what my day looked like:

6:15- Wake up, shower, shovel food in my face, and COFFEE
6:45- Wake my children up and get their breakfast ready
7:00-7:30- Get the kids ready for daycare
7:30- Leave for work
8:00- Early bird prep
8:40- Personal prep hour
9:30-3:30- Teach all day with no off-periods
3:30-5:30- Coach Speech Team or advise the Philanthropy Club
6:00- Get home and make dinner/play with the kids
7:00- Bathe the children and get them ready for bed
7:30- Stories and Bedtime
8:00-10:00- Grading and Lesson Prep
10:00-11:30- Graduate School Homework
11:30- Read or listen to my audiobook or just crash
AAANNND…Repeat.

Again, I don't share this with you to complain. Let me first say how grateful I was to have a job. I know SO many teachers who had to sub for years before getting hired on by a district. Second, my speech team salary filled in the financial gap between my ex-husband's internship stipend and our mortgage payment—so I had to be grateful for that. Finally, being a mom is the greatest thing that has ever happened to me. Period. My girls are the reason I kept going. But how LAME was it that I got so little time with them? Ok, maybe I needed to complain just a little bit...

What am I missing? Social time? Nonexistent. Exercise? Nope, that's not there. Time to run errands? Also not there. There are so many things I wished I could do during this time, but I just couldn't find a spare minute. Like so many of us, I was caught up in the newness of teaching, the newness of being a parent, and the stress that comes with both of those things.

Here's what I notice when I look at that schedule: I had ZERO time for any-thing I wasn't getting paid to do. I got paid to teach, I got paid to coach Speech, and a time-sensitive grant was paying for my graduate classes that year. (No won-der I didn't have any friends!) I made absolutely ZERO time for leisure activities. Looking back, it's a wonder I didn't struggle more with my mental health than I already did. While my schedule was super tight, I believe I could have done things differently, allowing myself a bit more breathing room in my daily life as a teacher and parent.

Using my experience as a teacher and parent who was stretched much too thin, I have restructured my life to include stricter boundaries, time for the things that bring me joy, and a significant increase in the time spent with my wonderful family. Finding time for these vital parts of my life have made me a better partner to my husband, a better mom to my girls, and a better teacher for my students. I no longer feel burnt out, and I no longer dread Monday mornings. I have made time for a life outside of school even though I am a dedicated teacher and a reflective practitioner, always looking for ways to grow as an educator. You can make time for it all too. Finding time for things that bring joy to our lives can help us avoid burning out, and can also help us bounce back if we're already feeling burnt out.

I've told you stories of some really awesome students, but I feel that it is important to share stories of when things went wrong. Because we all know that every day of teaching is not sunshine and rainbows. Teaching is hard. I know that is an oversimplified understatement, but you know what I mean. We did not choose an easy career. For many of us, we do more than "just teach." We coach or we advise a club at school, or we have a part-time job at a local restaurant, or we volunteer at our church, or we shuttle our children around town every night because they are in ALL THE ACTIVITIES. Regardless of what it is that we do beyond teaching, our days are full.

I think we signed up for a busy life when we decided to be teachers, but that doesn't make it easier when our non-teacher friends can do social things during the week when we are scrambling to get those tests graded, or get those lesson plans ready, or prepare for that observation that's coming up next week. Even when all of that is done, our minds are still busy. You know those students we mentally and emotionally take home with us? Yeah, they keep our brains busy. We think about what they are up to (are they getting into trouble?), whether or not they ate supper tonight, if someone is helping them with their homework, why their parents don't see how awesome they are…the list goes on. At school, at home, in the car, and wherever we go, our "teacher lives" can sneak up on us and keep us occupied. This mental toll plays a huge role in teacher burnout rates.

"Other Duties as Assigned"

Have you ever been "volun-told" to do something? (Volun-told (definition): an "opportunity" assigned to you by someone in authority over you, framed as a volunteer position) I sure have. As a second-year teacher, I was volun-told to lead a club centered around philanthropy and teaching students about local non-profits. It was a super cool group, but not at all what I needed with two babies at home and a speech team to build from scratch. Needless to say, I was worried about time. But my principal was awesome…

My principal at the time was one of those administrators who ALWAYS sided with his teachers. He would go to bat for us every time, even when we knew some parents were making his job very difficult. It was because of this that he had the respect of nearly every staff member in the building, along with most of the students. I had so much respect for this man. So when he "offered" me this "opportunity" to advise the philanthropy club, how could I say no? He took a chance hiring me—a brand new teacher—and he was thrilled when I announced my pregnancy, even when my maternity leave would fall during my very first year of teaching. He even covered the last 15 minutes of class himself occasionally so I could get to my OB appointments. He was a great guy. Therefore, I couldn't say no when he asked me to take on another task.

A little background: I was teaching at a large, public high school that year. I taught 3 sections of 9th grade English and a two-period block of an intervention-level English course. My students had limited computer access, so all of my grading was on paper. I lugged home a crate of papers to grade because I was still convinced I needed to grade ALL THE THINGS in order to be a good teacher. I had two little ones at home, a 6-month-old and an 18-month-old who spent their days with a nanny. My ex-husband was doing an internship that didn't pay enough to cover our daycare expenses, let alone our mortgage. I was also taking continuing education credits to try to earn a pay raise the next year.

Guess what? I didn't have time to take on anything else, But, you guessed it, I did it anyway. In retrospect, I should have told him "thank you, but no," but I didn't have it in me at the time. Since then, I have SLOWLY started to learn to say "no." It's not easy though, is it? Many teachers are people-pleasers. We like to make others happy and lessen their burdens. We are willing to go out of our way to help those in need, regardless of our own needs and wants. I am totally guilty of that. So what do we do?

1. **Set limits**

   Setting limits is crucial in finding balance. This can look different for each of us. For me, that might look like me not taking on any new after school activities. Or it might be only bringing home grading/lesson plans 3 nights a week and leaving everything at school on the other nights. For you, it might mean zero extra duties because your family needs you home right away after school. Or maybe you don't grade everything your students do; perhaps you just pick and choose what to grade. Whatever it is for you, find your limit and stick to it. Yes, there are going to be weeks where things like parent-teacher conferences, required professional development, or IEP/504 meetings keep you beyond your "normal" day, but try to avoid deviating from this plan as much as possible. You are only human after all. You have limits, and others (and you) need to respect those boundaries. In so many other professions, these limits are expected and understood. It is not unreasonable for teachers to follow suit. You would expect a doctor, a pilot, or any other professional with whom you work to set limits in order to maintain the quality of their work. It is important to hold yourself to the same standard.

2.   **Learn to say "no"**

This one is tough for me. Saying "no" to people, especially those I respect greatly, is difficult for me. I especially struggle with this because I fear that if I don't say "yes" to opportunities and prove myself when they come around, they won't ask again. I worry about not appearing to be a "team player," I worry about creating conflict with my supervisors, I worry about not appearing to be a good teacher. Needless to say, I worry a lot. But I worry because I care. I care about my family, my job, and my students. I want to be the best I can be, but it is so important to remember that we cannot be our best when we are stretched too thin. That's why I, and all of you, need to learn to say "no" when saying "yes" would create undue pressure and stress for you that might take away from the other things you have to do.

I'm sure we all know those superhuman teachers that appear to have it all together. You know the type: the ones with the perfect classroom décor and the amazing and time-consuming lesson plans; the ones who never seem to have a hair out of place. These super-teachers also seem to work out every day, coordinate their outfits so it looks like they have a never-ending closet, and appear to lack the caffeine addiction many of us deal with. I don't know how they do it. Maybe they are super-human, or maybe they only take on what they know they can rock at. Rather than be jealous of these teachers, I'm trying to follow their example to only take on as much as I can do well. I know I'm no super-teacher, but if I only take on what I can proudly accomplish, I am setting myself up for success, rather than a crash-and-burn-style failure.

3.   **Be ok with not pleasing everyone**

Are there any other people-pleasers in the room? It's not just me? Oh, thank goodness…I have a need to make other people happy. I don't know why. I just do. I find it very difficult to do things or make decisions that will make others unhappy. It was because of this need that I withheld the fact that I was getting a divorce for as long as I did. I was afraid people would say I was doing the wrong thing. But then I realized that it is also important to make myself happy because an unhappy person can only give so much at work and at home. I wasn't giving enough as a teacher, as a mother, as a person, because I was keeping myself in an unhappy place. Once I came to that realization, I was finally able to move on with my life and start growing as a person. Suddenly, work seemed less stressful, my lesson plans got done faster, and I was a WAY better mom. I had to be ok with not pleasing everyone and doing what I needed to do in order to be happy.

Pause for Reflection:

What limits can you set for yourself to ensure you are stretched too thin?

What does this mean for teachers?

Teachers are notoriously asked to do too much. The to-do list never seems to get shorter, in fact, more and more is added to our plates all the time. I know this isn't the most popular response, but here's the deal: as long as you keep teaching and assessing student learning, follow the rules, and stay open to accommodating the needs of your students and school, you're going to be just fine. You don't have to run the concession stand or staff the school carnival or chaperone the dance to be a good teacher. You don't need to volunteer to tutor for free or go to every single activity your students are in. You really don't. Is it nice when you can do those things every once in a while? Of course, it is, but it is not—and should not—be an expectation. Yes, your students love seeing your face in the crowd at every basketball game and band concert, but if not going will help you feel more together, remember, it is ok to not make everyone happy. Your students know you care even if you don't chaperone the Homecoming dance or show up at their piano recital. Don't worry about pleasing everyone, no matter how hard that can be. Good teachers have lives too. You don't need to feel guilty about focusing on your life outside of school, in fact, you should celebrate it.

CHAPTER 6

Everyone Else Who Needs You

When I was a college student, I burnt out more than once. Unlike many of the people in my life, my college years weren't spent with friends having fun, nor were they spent throwing myself into my studies. During this time in my life, I let myself get pulled in way too many directions to the point where I felt I wasn't doing anything well.

After classes and work, I stayed up all night doing homework, getting anywhere between two and four hours of sleep. I was fueled by Rockstar Punched, coffee, and the little voice inside my head that told me I could be better. I lost touch with my friends and roommates, I stopped taking care of myself physically, and my mental health spiraled out of control. I got stuck in the monotony of my daily life consisting of two on-campus jobs, music lessons, choir, theatre, and the overload of classes I told myself I could handle. Needless to say, no one got the best version of me during that time.

But apparently, I was a glutton for punishment. Whenever another student worker needed me to pick up a shift, I did it. When I was put in groups for large projects, I took on a leadership role without questioning it. There simply were not enough hours in the day for me to do everything I had on my to-do list and stay healthy and sane.

Fortunately for me, or unfortunately depending on how you look at it, my body let me know that this course of action was just not going to fly. I got sick, like really sick, to the point where I couldn't do it all for a few days. I finally slept, and my body and mind got a much-needed break from it all.

I wish I could say that I learned my lesson and am now living a stress-free life, but that wouldn't be true. I did, however, learn that even my own ambition for success has a limit, and that reaching this limit means I am no good for anyone, least of all myself. All of the people who were counting on me: my professors, my classmates, my co-workers, my friends, my roommates, and so on, were not getting what they needed from me. I needed to step back and get some perspective on how I was living my life. Through that experience, I learned so much about myself and my own limitations. These lessons still serve as reminders to slow down and make sure that I don't take on more than I can handle.

Have any of you ever done one of those thankfulness challenges? The ones where you list all of the people and things you are grateful for? Well, I have, and my family and friends are right at the top of my list. I've never been the kind of person who has a ton of friends. It takes a lot for me to truly connect with other people, and I think that's why the people I've let in are so important to me. The awesome people I have befriended over the years are like family.

Pause to Reflect:

I want to challenge you to do this right now. In your Reflection journal or here in your book, I want you to write ten people or things you are grateful for today. They can be big things or little things, there are no wrong answers.

What does a list like this mean for me? It means that if the people on my list need me, I'm there. No questions asked. I've picked people up at three in the morning when they don't have money for an Uber. I have stayed on the phone for hours while also taking care of my kids. I've baked last-minute birthday cakes in the middle of the night for my friend's kid and loved every minute of it. Teachers are notorious for taking on extras like this. But these extras aren't just things on a to-do list, they come with complicated and sometimes draining friendships. When we have other people who need us, whether those people are our spouses, our children, our other family members, or our friends, our to-do list gets longer, and our extras just keep piling up.

Your list of who needs you might be different than mine. Perhaps you help care for a neighbor, or you have a sickly pet, or maybe you volunteer at your church or another community organization. All of those people are important, but so are you. If not to yourself, then you sure are to all of them, whether they tell you or not.

I think we all have had people in our lives that drain our batteries more than they help us recharge. But shouldn't our friends help us feel whole again? That's what I hope for in my friendships. Unfortunately, some people need a counselor (which I am not) instead of a friend and frankly, I don't always know how to help them. We all have people that need us to lift them up, and there is nothing wrong with that every once in a while, but there is no tired like teacher tired and sometimes we just can't do it, even when we want to. Remember earlier when I mentioned that we cannot fill other people's cups when ours are empty? This is something that MANY teachers need to remember. It isn't easy to admit, but we are not super-human. We need to refill our own metaphorical cups every now and again.

But how can we do this when we have students, family, friends, neighbors, and others who need us every day? Their needs don't go away when we're running on empty. I wish I had a magical solution to this problem for everyone, but alas, I do not. For me, I have realized that I need to set limits on what I can give to others. What does that look like? I have decided that I will help those who need me, but there has to be a point when I stop helping them. Picture with me a kid learning to ride a bike. At first, they need training wheels to help them (I'm the training wheels in this metaphor). Then, they can take the training wheels off, but they need help keeping their balance (Now I'm the adult helping them keep their balance). Finally, all they need is a little push to get started, but then they are on their own (That's me letting them go).

This gradual release model is something nearly all teachers use in their classrooms, but many of us forget that it can also be applied in our personal lives outside of school as well.

Since I've come to that realization, I've made changes to how I approach my friends and family when they need help. Now, when I agree to help my family or friends with a crisis or struggle they are experiencing, instead of just slapping a Band-Aid on the problem and moving on (which is the quick fix—the "easier option"), I try to help them come to the solution themselves so that, in the future, they can help themselves instead of needing to lean on me to fix things for them. That may sound harsh or unsympathetic, but I'd rather be the fun friend than the fix-it friend. Being the fix-it friend all of the time is exhausting and it makes that friendship become work for me instead of a mutually beneficial relationship. By helping my friends grow and learn to help themselves, I can preserve that friendship as something that gives me joy and helps me recharge.

I know that discussing our interpersonal relationships with other people, especially other adults, is a bit out of character for a teacher book, but stick with me here. If you are the fix-it friend, as I have been, this can seriously weigh on you. It can affect your ability to do your job, to be a good parent, to be a good partner. So what do we do when we have been put in this position? When we are the one people want in their lives for when they need something? How can we first, reconcile the fact that those in our lives are using us as a Band-Aid, and then move forward to a place where we can advocate for ourselves?

You guys, this is so hard. As teachers, we love to fix things, whether it's helping a kid *finally* understand that math concept, or helping a student get the resources they need because they aren't having their basic needs met, or being there for a friend in need as they cope with whatever is causing them stress. It's like we're wired for this. It's as if we're programmed to turn off our own needs and wants and stresses to take care of everyone else.

I have seen this in action. I have seen my closest friend, who is also a teacher, with more than enough on her own plate take on organizing a club for a group of students who are regularly overlooked, get a part-time job to help her family pay the bills, take in foster children, and still manage to crush it as an educator. And she did it without hesitation, without a thought of how it would affect her personally. We all do this. We put others before ourselves in ways both big and small all the time. This happens at school, as we all know, but do we see it when these tendencies creep into our personal lives?

Confession time, I am the worst at this. Most of it is my inner teacher's tendency to try to fix everything, but it also stems from my desire to please the people in my life. I have driven my sweet husband crazy with my constant concern for his mood and my need to make him smile, like all the time. He has to remind me all the time that sometimes work is just stressful for him and that he doesn't need me to fix it. I have been known to go on elaborate baking or crafting kicks with my kids because one of them will say that I spent a lot of time working that week and not much time playing dolls with them. I will buy my friends gifts for no reason at all because I'm afraid I haven't been a good enough friend lately. Seriously, I'm the worst at boundaries sometimes.

So what do we all need to remember when these fix-it tendencies crop up again and again? What can we do to save ourselves from a downward spiral because everyone needs us? It's easier said than done, I know, but we have to find perspective. Here's how I do it:

- If I'm feeling like I haven't been a good enough partner to my husband, I do a check-in (instead of missing the mark and buying him a present or something like that). I'll ask, what do you need from me this week, or is there anything I can do to better support you this week? We talk it through, and usually, that's all he needs. He doesn't need or want the gift in my Etsy cart, he usually just wants me to be present with him and not stuck in teacher-mode.
- If I'm feeling like my kids aren't getting the best version of me, I put everything else aside, even if I'm under a deadline, and I ask them what they need from me. Usually, they just want to play a board game or have me read them a story, but sometimes, they just want me to stop and hug them for as long as they need. We both feel rejuvenated and I feel reconnected with my kids.
- If I feel I'm failing my friends because I've turned them down for coffee or drinks or trivia one too many times, I call them and just let them tell me about what is going on in their lives. I ask them about things in their lives that bring them joy, whether that's their kids or coaching or crafting or whatever, and we both can leave the conversation feeling like a weight of guilt has been taken off our shoulders.

Ok, so I know these things are no-brainers for many of you. I'm sure that there are some of you who are super well-adjusted and have their friendships and other interpersonal relationships under control. If that's you, I'm so happy for you. If you're like me though, you might need the reminder. The act of writing this chapter is my reminder. I hope that by reading it, it will be yours.

If, like me, the friends in your life are limited to a select few, just remember that while they may need you, and your family may need you, and your neighbor may need you, and your students may need you, *you also need you too*. You need to be there for yourself, just like you are for everyone else who needs you. Being a teacher is a unique position to be in as a friend, a partner, and a family member. The pressures on us are different than those who work your typical 9-5 job.

We don't fall into that "normal" category. We have unique challenges in our work lives that make our interpersonal relationships tough at times. I don't know about you, but I'm so thankful for the people in my life who accept me and my crazy teacher life the way I am. We all just need to remember to keep ourselves near the top of our "people who need us" lists, because if we don't, we won't be able to be there for everyone else.

CHAPTER 7

Self-Care?

Before my wedding, I decided to indulge in a little bit of self-care. This wasn't my normal sit-on-the-couch-with-a-glass-of-wine-and-some-nachos-and-binge-watch-Downton-Abbey kind of self-care. No. I thought I'd try the kind of self-care I see praised on social media and in self-help books for women in order to "beautify" myself before my big day. Like many brides-to-be, I read articles on getting ready for my wedding, and nearly all of the sites I visited touted the importance of the pre-wedding beauty products and services. Now, I didn't go all out like some women do; I didn't crash diet or visit a dermatologist for a year or anything like that. However, I did push myself a bit outside of my comfort zone, just for something new. I tried face masks, special bubble baths, hair masks, a pedicure, and a massage. I figured that a pre-wedding pampering session was in order because I had never tried it and I thought it was a good excuse.

I hate to break it to you, but it wasn't long before I was so bored with it all. Sure, the pedicure was lovely and the massage felt nice, but I missed my nachos and that sassy Dowager Countess! I had thought that my version of self-care was lacking something because it wasn't anything special, but I was so wrong. I love binge-watching television shows with my husband. I love playing board games and having a glass of wine after a stressful day at school. Sure, I'll probably still get the occasional pedicure, but I learned that my version of self-care is just as valid as the fancy kind. My nachos and wine do the same thing for me as someone else's face mask and manicure.

Taking care of yourself is crucial to a happy and long-lasting career as a teacher. I learned that I don't need to do what everyone else is doing for it to "count" as self-care. As long as I am caring for myself enough to stay an engaged teacher, parent, *and partner, it doesn't matter if I'm relaxing on the couch or baking cookies with my kids, it all counts as self-care.*

Okay guys, let's get real. People have been preaching about the importance of self-care for a long time, but while I can fully recognize that self-care is important (remember my mini-rant about filling our own cups so we can fill others'?), I just don't know how some people do it. I work with some amazing teachers who are also parents and coaches who find time for 5 CrossFit workouts a week. I know teachers who never bring anything home from school and who have actual hobbies. Some of my colleagues can meal prep for every meal of the week. Others play multiple sports. Some read 75 books a year, just for fun! These people seem superhuman to me, but the ones that really get me are the teachers who do all of the above and still come to school looking like they just stepped out of a salon. I know, I know, that's super shallow of me, but I just don't know how they do it.

I am a full-time teacher, full-time mom, and I am usually advising at least one school activity. I have only taught the same class two years in a row *one time*, so I'm constantly locating or creating curriculum materials. My children have activities multiple times a week and are too young to just be dropped off. I have a wonderful husband with whom I like to spend as much of my free time as I can. I have attempted to maintain healthy friendships, eat well enough so I have the energy to get through my day, and be physically active so I can sleep at night; however, I no longer have time to work out like I used to. I don't even read half of the books I add to my bookshelves. I can't remember the last time I got a haircut. My house is a mess. My instruments are collecting dust in my living room. I'm going grey and my stress level is contributing greatly to my adult acne and coffee addiction. I am stressed out most of the time.

You may be thinking that you are even busier than me, and you might be right. Maybe I have no reason to rant about my stress level, but I think that each of us has our own definition of stressed out. For some, my life would be a piece of cake. For others, everything I do may seem totally overwhelming. My life is busy and stressful and full of activity, but it's also pretty great. Sure, there are days where I threaten to sell a student for a Diet Coke because I just can't deal, but most days are pretty wonderful.

I am lucky to be a mom to two amazingly awesome little girls who make my life worth all of the stress and tiredness. I have the most supportive and loving partner in life who lets me cry and laugh and tell teacher stories until I can't even remember why I was upset in the first place. I am super fortunate to work with a group of students who are so witty and clever and hilarious. My administrators really care about our students and support our staff. All in all, I love my life.

Although, if any teachers/parents are reading this book, I think you'll understand where I'm coming from when I tell you that self-care is like #11 on my list of Top Ten Priorities. But that's not a healthy way to be, and I know that. Unfortunately, knowing that I need to do something like taking care of myself doesn't make it easier. So what do I do about it? Well, I'm not an expert on self-care, but I do know that self-care can simply be doing the things that help you recharge or feel at peace. For me, that can mean writing for an hour after the kids go to bed even when there is laundry to fold or a dishwasher that needs to be unloaded. It can mean listening to an audiobook with my husband, working on our puzzle, and not doing anything else. Sometimes, I go to bed when my girls do and leave the housework and the grading for the next day. Or maybe I'll venture out and play trivia with a friend on a Monday night instead of bringing my computer home to lesson plan.

As you can see, my version of self-care is not exactly glamorous. I don't get weekly manicures or monthly massages or go on mini-vacations to get away from the stressful parts of my life. I find that simple things like closing my computer and recharging my batteries by getting some extra sleep or watching an episode of *Friends* after the kids go to sleep can help reduce my stress and set me up to be more productive the next day. By taking time to do things that bring us peace, we can become better and happier teachers.

So what can you do to practice self-care? Think about the things that bring you joy. Is it cooking a big meal? Is it reading a book in the tub? Is it letting out some frustration at the gym? Is it working on your latest craft project? Whatever it is, it is a valid way to practice self-care. Maybe you haven't found your "thing" yet, and that is also totally okay. What's important to remember is that all of us are human and if we don't recharge once in a while, we can burn out.

Pause for reflection:

What is your self-care go-to? What can you do to make time for that activity this month?

After my fourth year of teaching, I burnt out. As in I literally felt like a failure and I almost quit for good. That year is one I look back on and cringe. My mental health had taken a serious dive. That year, I was traveling between schools which meant I felt I couldn't give either school my best. My personal life was a mess. I felt like I was failing my own children and I didn't know how to pull myself out of the dark place in which I found myself. I was miserable. You know that feeling when you find yourself stretched so thin that you can't do anything well? That was me in year four.

I remembered reading somewhere that half of all new teachers burn out or quit within their first five years. When I got my first job, I promised myself I wouldn't be a part of that statistic. But there I was, burnt out and ready to leave it all behind. I wanted a different job, but there wasn't anything that wouldn't require me to move, which wasn't an option. At the time, I decided to leave education. I felt that I didn't have another option because frankly if I were on the other side of an interview with me, I wouldn't have hired myself.

In the end, I took a year-long leave of absence to focus on graduate school, which my district so graciously allowed. I stayed home with my youngest, taking her to preschool, swimming lessons, and storytime at the library. I recharged my batteries and learned how to be happy again.

This experience of staying home taught me something I really needed to learn. At the beginning of the year, I was crushed that I wasn't out school supply shopping for my classroom or decorating bulletin boards or lesson planning. When the first day of school came around, I felt like I had lost something huge. I was mourning a group of students I would never have the chance to teach and it hurt, so bad. As the weeks went on, I got into a new rhythm, but there was one thing that didn't go away: I missed school! I loved my time at home with my daughter, and I wouldn't trade that time for any-thing, but that wasn't my biggest takeaway from my leave of absence.

My biggest take-away was that a life outside a school was not for me. I missed the schedule, the consistency, the kids who counted on me. I missed working. So when job posting started appearing in late winter, I poured over them, looking for what could be a good fit for me. I found a middle school English position, and after a phone interview with the principal, I was back! I had a teaching job, doing something brand new to me, teaching middle school. And you guys, it's great!

Middle school students, who used to terrify me, are now my absolute favorite. They are funny and insightful and curious and willing to take risks.

They haven't learned to be "too cool for school yet," and most of them still sincerely want to please their teachers. We laugh, we are silly, and we have a lot of fun, but at the same time, we tackle tough topics and big questions. We learn together and I never have a dull day. I've loved it. Yes, I've moved schools since that first middle school position, but I'm still working with the greatest bunch of sixth-grade weirdos yet (yes, I say that every year). These students are something else.

So where does self-care fit in? Well, now that I know that I'm doing what I'm meant to do, working with middle school students, I needed to figure out how to do that without getting burnt out again. That is easier said than done, because sixth-graders, while awesome, are super demanding of a person's time and energy.

Each grade level is draining in a different way. Younger ones demand constant supervision, attention, and affirmations. Older students need to be reengaged and remotivated so often. And all of them need caring teachers who give everything they've got every day. So how can we provide our students with what they need while still taking care of ourselves? To oversimplify, I have learned to leave my work at work and my home life at home. I maximize my time in both places in order to find and maintain balance.

I have found a rhythm. I put my kids on the early bus so I have an hour to prep before school. I work through lunch and I use my prep time every single day. My kids are back to me within minutes of my last bell, and from then on, I'm Mom. My days are hectic and busy and full of learning and grading, but it works for me. I can leave my work in my classroom on most nights, and my husband and I get real quality time together nearly every day, which brings me such joy. No, it's not glamorous or particularly thrilling, but it is my way of bringing balance back to my life.

Your self-care may look completely different from mine, and that's awesome. Whatever you need to do to find balance, do it. To say this job is hard is a major understatement, and we need to take care of ourselves. So drink some water, move your body a bit, get out and be social, go home and read a book, do what you need to do to be the best version of you. It doesn't have to be fancy, it just has to be enough to give you a sense of balance and peace in the craziness of teacher life.

PART THREE

Our Priorities

'Education is not the filling of a pot but the lighting of a fire.'
—W.B. YEATS

CHAPTER 8

Who or what is most important?

The very first time I interviewed for teaching jobs, I tried to sell myself as a 100% all-in teacher who would put everything I had into the job if they would just give me the chance to show them. Now, years later, I look back on that and wonder what I was thinking.

Granted, I do tend to be an all-in person. When I'm at school, I try to give it my all. When I'm at home, I want to give my kids the best version of myself possible. When I take on a new project, I focus all of my energy on it. Being all-in can be a good thing until it becomes a liability.

When I throw myself into what I'm doing and block out everything else, that tunnel vision mentality often means that I neglect other areas in my life. When I treat my current task as the only important thing, I am often disappointed in my lack of follow-through elsewhere. For example, when I threw myself into grading in the hours after my children go to bed, I forgot to prepare their outfits for a dress-up day at school. I felt like a good teacher for getting the grading done, but like a bad mom for missing "Beach Day" for my kids. When I went all-in as a homeschooling-in-the-summer mom, my house was a disaster. I felt like I was doing a good thing for my kids, but failing as a homeowner.

When I reflect upon that first job interview, I wish I could go back and change my responses. Being 100% all-in at all times is simply not practical. When you are a teacher with a life outside of school, the two sometimes have to co-exist on your to-do list. At my latest job interview, I tried a different tactic. This time I didn't give them the answer I did when I first started. I didn't promise 100%

commitment to the job. I told them the truth. I have a clear priority system worked out that puts my family first, with no exceptions. I waited for them to react negatively, but instead, I was met with understanding and respect for my position as a working mom.

I learned that while schools want their teachers to be committed to their work, we aren't living in the early 1900s when schools wouldn't hire married teachers or teachers with lives outside of school. Schools want to maintain their teachers. They want us to feel fulfilled so we will stay on and continue teaching, even when our lives outside of school get busy. I have come to realize that being honest about who and what is most important to me has earned me respect and understanding from my employer.

Are there any other to-do list people out there? Not just me? Ok, good. Because I honestly don't know what I would do without my lists. It's oddly satisfying to cross things off, especially when they are things only you really notice have been completed. This is why I have always used two planners, one on paper for my checklist items, and one on my computer for meetings and other places to be. I know that probably sounds terribly inefficient, but it works for me. I need a to-do list on paper. I have tried online sticky notes and Google Keep lists on my phone, among other things, and it just doesn't give me the same feelings of accomplishment.

I have a confession to make. Sometimes, I'm even guilty of writing things down even after I have completed them just so I can cross them off my list. I have gone back and filled out missing planner pages just so I can see a list of things I've gotten done. I like seeing a list of completed tasks at the end of the day. It makes me feel accomplished.

There are days when I don't feel like I've achieved anything unless I see a long to-do list all crossed off. On those days, I am often disappointed, because if you know anything about a teacher's day, sometimes the things we have to do aren't on the list. Sometimes they aren't even in the job description. ("Other duties as assigned," right?) We can often get derailed during our prep periods by students needing homework help, colleagues needing to vent, or administrators wanting to check-in. Sometimes, I even find myself taking care of family things that will "only take a minute." I sign up for volunteering, plan out how we're going to make all of the activities work around my husband's and my schedule that week, and so on. All of those things are often valuable uses of our time, but they can come at the expense of the to-do lists we've so carefully crafted.

That poses the question, who or what is most important? In those moments when we find ourselves doing other things that we hadn't put on our to-do lists, should we zero in on those pre-assigned tasks, or do we need to rewrite our list to include the other things we feel are important?

I've read about people with separate work and home planners or lists. They can compartmentalize each set of tasks into a designated organizational system and in doing so, they seem to be able to truly separate work and home. For teachers though, I just don't see how that is possible, especially if you are also a parent.

Hypothetically, if I were going to truly separate work and school, I honestly don't know how I would accomplish everything I need to. Most days I do spend a few minutes of my prep emailing my kid's teachers, communicating with coaches, and coordinating our family schedule with my husband. I pay the occasional bill over lunch and plan meals for the week when I can. I also get my grading done, my lesson plans written, and my copies made during that time.

So for me, one big to-do list is the way to go. I can juggle everything in those few minutes to myself during the day and then when I get home, I get to be Mom, without having to sacrifice that time to do all of the things I need to do to run our household. Sure the laundry, dishes, and other chores are awaiting me at home, but my family can do those things together, making the most of our family time.

If you are like me, you probably do a combination of these things because you are being pulled in many different directions. The key is to narrow your focus to who or what is most important. That leads us to the question: what are our priorities, and how can they help guide our days and focus our energy?

I know that priorities are often very personal as each of us places a different amount of importance on each aspect of our lives. Some of you may live and breathe school. That's awesome. Some of you may live your life in the car, shuttling kids around. That's awesome. Some of you may not know what your priorities are yet. That's awesome, too. I was feeling that way too very recently. I felt torn between being a good teacher, a good mom, a good partner to my husband, all while trying to take care of myself. Needless to say, I couldn't keep all of those things going at 100%.

So, what did I do? I let one slip. I let myself slip. I felt that it was completely unacceptable to me to be anything less than my best at being a mom, a teacher, and a partner. So I stopped exercising regularly. I ate quick convenient food that didn't sustain my energy level. I wore my hair in a braid or a top knot almost daily because I couldn't justify spending time on my appearance. I subbed coffee for meals and then ate junk during my preps. I used to pride myself on my quirky, nerdy teacher dresses, and I stopped wearing them because I didn't feel comfortable in my own skin. My house was a disaster. I couldn't find my desk. I quit writing, and I didn't read a book for fun for months. I was exhausted from keeping all of those plates spinning.

Finally, one day, my husband asked me what he could do for me. He saw how stressed and anxious I had become and, being the awesome man that he is, he wanted to help. That one little question sent me over the edge. I started ugly crying (embarrassing, I know). I vented about all of the things around the house that I needed to do, and how I felt I would never get all of these papers graded, and how I felt gross because I wasn't taking care of myself. I felt awful, and I'm sure it wasn't a pretty thing to behold.

He comforted me and asked if he could take some things off of my plate. And the next night I came home to him folding two loads of laundry in the *clean* living room and the sound of the dishwasher running in the *clean* kitchen. I started to cry all over again (poor guy). I thanked him over and over, but he said he was just trying to lighten my load a bit. He reminded me that he (and other people) cannot read my mind and that I just need to ask when I need help.

Asking for help is and has always been one of my weaknesses. I always think I should be able to do it myself, and I don't want to burden anyone else. But since that day, I've been trying to be better. I am not a super mom, a super teacher, or a superwoman. I am human, and sometimes, I need help. And I need to balance my priorities so that I don't leave myself behind.

I decided that I needed to find balance again. To do that, I needed to redefine my priorities to give me some clarity, because what I was doing was clearly not working. I couldn't continue to function in that way.

Here's how I broke down my priorities:

1. I prioritize my family. They are first, always.
2. I prioritize being a dynamic teacher.
3. I prioritize my personal goals and dreams.

As you can see, my list is pretty small. The things that are super important to me fall into those three categories. If I were looking at my situation from the outside, I would probably give myself the following advice: If the thing I'm considering taking on doesn't fit into one of those three categories, it probably shouldn't be a priority. I can still do it if I have time, but only the things that serve to support my big three categories should become priorities.

You may notice that having a spotless house is not on that list. Neither is losing weight. And nowhere on that list is anything about being perfect. Perfection is not attainable, but progress is. I encourage you to write down your priorities and only give your all to the things on that list. That way, you can focus on what's most important and do those things well. Keeping too many plates spinning can lead to a disaster, so don't forget to breathe, ask for help if you need it, and always keep your priorities in mind.

Now it's your turn. What are your priorities?

Pause to Reflect:

If you had to come up with a list of your top three priorities, what would be on there?

For some, your list may look very similar to mine. For others, you may have entirely different things you need to prioritize right now. Whatever is on your list, I want to challenge you to use those things to guide your decisions.

Maybe your list needs to be longer than mine. Perhaps you are in a place where you can focus on five priorities or even ten. If so, that's amazing, and I aspire to get to that place someday. But I want to caution you before you try to tackle a list that long. Start small, perhaps with three things on your list like me. Then, if you find balance working towards those things, start to slowly add things to it.

While I know that our teaching jobs are not always at the top of our priority lists (my job isn't my number one priority), it is important to at least have it on the list. That way, we are setting ourselves up to thrive both in and out of school. I encourage you to make being a good teacher a priority. Notice that I didn't say a *perfect* teacher. You don't have to be perfect to be good at this job. You just need to find balance with your other priorities in order to become more centered and more able to do everything you need to do well.

CHAPTER 9

What do I have to do to be a "good teacher"?

*H*ave you ever had one of those students with whom, no matter how hard you tried, you just didn't click? One of my former students was like that for me. He portrayed himself as disinterested in pretty much everything we did. He never got excited about things, he would question every single assignment and could be downright rude to me in front of his classmates. Now, he's a bright kid who could easily have earned a 4.0 if he had wanted to, but school was clearly not his passion.

I asked the other teachers on my team, and they had very similar experiences with him. I reached out to administrators, our counselor, and even a former teacher of his to try to find out what I could do to encourage him. Nothing came of those conversations, and I felt really defeated. I pride myself on the relationships I'm able to form with my students, but it just wasn't happening with this young man.

A few weeks later, I was at my daughter's swimming lessons. All of the other parents were on their phones, so I found myself wandering. I started reading the records board and was surprised when I saw my student's name up there, not once, but three times! He had set and held records over the past few years. A lightbulb went off in my head. I'd found it! I'd found the thing I could use to connect with him!

The next day, I jokingly said to him, "You didn't tell me you were a record-winning swimmer!" He looked at me like I had lost it. But I went on to describe the records board I had looked at the night before. All of a sudden, his demeanor changed. He stood a little taller and told me that the board was missing another *one of his records he had set that season. I made a really big deal about his accomplishments and asked him to keep me posted on the rest of his season.*

I thought I had done it. I thought our relationship would be forever changed. Alas, my silly naïve self would soon be disappointed. Nothing changed! He and I still had the same old awkward rapport which made me feel even more defeated. It was a few days later that I had resigned myself to the fact that it probably wasn't going to happen. But then, he surprised me.

We had just gotten done with a really fun project in class when I received an email from him. I braced myself for criticism; however, I was pleasantly surprised. He said he really enjoyed the project and that he hoped we'd do another one like it soon. I was over the moon! I emailed him back thanking him and promising more things like that before the year was through.

Was that student relationship tough to tackle? You bet it was. But it was so worth it. I had done it. He started slowly showing interest in our classes, and our conversations turned much more positive. That relationship was one that meant the most that year. Would it win me any sort of recognition? Nope. But that's not what it's about. Succeeding in developing that relationship helped me feel like a good teacher.

I have been haunted by the perfection demonstrated by teachers on Pinterest and Teachers Pay Teachers since the first day I fell down the rabbit hole of teacher blogs and social media for teachers. I look at their immaculate classrooms and their graphic-designer-esque handouts and feel like a slacker. I think, *how could any human being accomplish all of that? Don't they have lives outside of school?* That vision of being a perfect teacher seems so out of reach, but yet, I have always imagined what it would be like to do what they do.

I will dream up a classroom theme and design plan. I make one awesome looking handout or plan one elaborate lesson. I will meal plan a list of perfectly balanced lunches and snacks. I will clean my classroom until it shines like the first day of school all over again. And then reality sets in. I want the end product that would come with being that put-together, Pinterest-worthy teacher, but frankly, I do not have the drive nor do I have the time to become one. It's just not on my priority list. Do I have the skills required to produce worksheets that look like that for every lesson I teach? Yep. But I also have two kids and a house to clean. Could I pour more of my own time and money into my classroom to make it look like those designer rooms I covet on social media? Sure I could. But again, I am fortunate enough to have lots to keep me busy once that final bell rings, and quite honestly, this teacher's pockets just aren't that deep.

So how do I reconcile the kind of teacher I am in reality with the dream version of my teacher self? How can I be ok using other teacher's ideas, lesson plans, and handouts when I know that I am perfectly capable of creating things like them myself? Am I really content with my boring classroom décor after seeing the awesomeness that exists down the hall from me?

I have struggled with these questions since year one when I survived on Teachers Pay Teachers and my mentor teacher's filing cabinet. I felt lucky to get through the day without needing to have a good cry during my prep (note: I was also pregnant during my first year of teaching, so cut me some slack). So how do I do it? I embrace the aspects of my job that I do well and find peace with the things I simply cannot do. That doesn't mean I'm ok with slacking off or not putting in the work it takes to do my job. It just means that I focus on what actually matters to me and to my students: the relationships. I pour my heart and soul into letting those little goofballs know that I've got their back, pure and simple. The lesson planning and everything else is secondary. My students don't really care if the escape room we just did was purchased during the last Teachers Pay Teachers cyber sale. They are ok with my "go with the flow" seating charts. They just want a teacher who cares about them.

Yes, this is an over-simplification, and yes it probably means I don't have a "Teacher of the Year" nomination in my future, but honestly, I don't care. What I do care about are those students who come into my room every day. All of them are constantly reminded that my room is a safe place for them and that the invitation to really push themselves to their potentials will always be there.

I tell them on the first day of school each year that I know I won't be the best teacher they ever have, but I promise to care for them Every. Single. Day. No exceptions. I will care about them, their fantasy football rants, their obscure meme references, and their constant TikTok talk. I will see them as people first and students second. I will make them work to earn their grades, and I will cheer them on as they chase their goals. I will challenge them to think differently, to be kind, and to be the best version of themselves possible—no exceptions. I also try to walk the walk. I am honest about my mistakes, I own up to not having all of the answers, and I let them see me fail, only to try again and do better next time. I talk to them about my goals and let them teach me new things. Am I perfect? Absolutely not. Do I have off days?

You bet I do. But I try to wipe the slate clean and start each day with a growth mindset and a smile for each student as they walk in my room.

At the end of the day, I am not the dream version of my teacher self. My desk is a disaster most days, and I sometimes even lesson plan on Monday mornings before school. I don't always grade papers as quickly as I should, and run on WAY too much coffee and my secret snack stash. But what I can offer these kids is, in my opinion, more important than a perfectly organized classroom and elaborately planned lessons every day. I can offer them a teacher who genuinely likes her job and who sincerely cares about each of them. I can offer them a cheerleader, a school mom, and an advocate. And all of that is how I know I am a good teacher.

So what does this mean for you?

It means you, like me, need to cut yourself some slack! Those "perfect" teachers out there are either cyborgs, or they aren't as perfect as we think they are. I'll bet we all tidy up a bit more when we know we have an evaluation coming up. I try to imagine those perfect pictures on social media as snapshots of a career-making evaluation day. I'll bet it gets messed up later. I'll bet they had to clear some clutter before taking those pictures. I'll bet they have boxes of junk hidden somewhere else ready to pour out of a closet, cartoon-style (or else they are besties with Marie Kondo. If that's the case, and you know her, please send her my way!).

What I'm saying is this: perfection in the long term is not practical. Perfection should not be the goal. It's like I tell my students, the goal should be to learn more and get a little bit better every day. The goal should not be perfection. When perfection is the goal, we will fall short every single time. We're human. As long as we're moving forward and doing our best, we're succeeding.

I'm sure some of you have a flair for organization and your classroom is always neat and tidy. I'll bet among you is an aspiring interior designer whose classroom is a work of art. I'm sure at least one of you has a booming Teachers Pay Teachers store. Some of you may have been nominated for Teacher of the Year. I'll bet among you is a future YouTube teacher sensation (that's a thing, right?). But I'll bet very few of you are *all* of those things. Some of you are probably parents of busy kids who would agree that you are the best parent ever (even if they won't say it out loud). Most of you probably have a friend who wouldn't know what to do without you. Nearly all of us have other people and places that require our attention, and we have to be ok with that. I know that it sounds hypocritical of me as a recovering self-critic, but it is ok to not be a perfect teacher. With everything else we need to do and be as humans, it's improbable that we will be masters at everything we do.

We need to accept that fact. We need to accept our shortcomings and celebrate the things we're good at. Maybe you're super good at bringing games into your classroom but writing tests just isn't your strength. That's ok, you're still a good teacher. Perhaps you're the teacher every kid knows will be their rock in times of trouble, but you're still teaching out of a 20-year-old textbook because you don't have time to recreate the wheel. That's ok, you're still a good teacher. Maybe you're everyone's go-to for technology help or curriculum design, but you never bring anything home because your family time is precious to you. That's ok, you're still a good teacher.

What I'm trying to say is that even though none of us are perfect at everything, we are still good teachers. We care. We listen. We learn from our mistakes and are trying to improve every day. Are we the teachers of our dreams? Maybe not. But I can promise you that for at least one of your kids, you are the teacher of theirs.

Pause for Reflection:

What are your strengths as a teacher? List three things you do well.

Finish this sentence: I am a good teacher because _____

CHAPTER 10

What do I get out of this?

A *few months ago, my students and I were discussing what they believe to be a necessity in their lives: their AirPods. They couldn't believe I've never owned a pair, nor that I have never considered purchasing a set. I thought, this is the perfect opportunity for a real-world conversation. I told them that while they are really cool, and I'm sure super convenient, they cost the same amount as a month of my children's piano lessons. They just sort of blinked at me. They couldn't imagine not getting something they wanted because of the cost. Most of my students at this school come from fairly affluent families, so not being able to afford something just wasn't a part of their lives. There's also the fact that none of them support a household on their income, but that's par for the course for most students.*

To put this into a little bit of context, I switched schools this year. I now work at a private school that is MUCH closer to my home and offers me some terrific benefits for my children. However, I make less money than I did before. Like, significantly less. So when my students suggested that I go buy a set of expensive headphones when the ones I already own work perfectly well, my immediate response was, I can't afford them, and even if I could, they're not in the budget.

At the moment, I teased my students about their "First World" responses (an on-going joke in my room), but later I thought about it some more and I realized that moment was just another reminder that I don't earn very much money for the work I do. Yes, I earn enough to provide all of my family's basic needs, plus some extras such as dance and piano lessons for my children, and frankly, there isn't much I want beyond what I already have. But little things my non-teacher friends do, such as travel or drive new cars, are not a part of my reality. While I knew that going into teaching, as we all did, I still think many of us with our naïve views of the world as new college graduates didn't see these feelings coming. We saw teaching as a natural choice, a way to commit our lives to helping kids learn more and reach their potential. While that is a beautiful sentiment, it doesn't always help us feel better when our non-teacher friend doesn't have to shop the clearance rack, has those AirPods our students love, or goes out to lunch every day because they make more money than we do. They simply have more disposable income than teachers have.

I know, I know, we're not supposed to talk about money in this way. We're supposed to say that we're grateful for our salaries and that we're lucky to have steady jobs, but sometimes, that's really tough. How can we feel that when the world around us is screaming at us to "treat ourselves" and we just can't? Our society has become more materialistic, and the urge is definitely there to jump on that bandwagon, but as we all know, we signed up for a job without a big paycheck. We signed up for a job that would allow us to share our love of school and of learning with our students.

I'm sure all of us have had moments like this in our teaching careers when we think about the things/experiences/etc. we could purchase if we made more money. Maybe we'd travel more, get monthly massages, treat ourselves to a Starbucks more often, or something else along those lines. We all know that teaching is not the career to choose if one is looking to be rich. I see very few teachers driving brand-new cars (except for those for whom that is a priority) and I hear many young teachers dreaming of the day they don't have student loans to repay. This can be extremely challenging to explain to the people around us. I don't know about you, but I find that I need to justify my frustrations about salary negotiations and the like because my non-teacher friends think I'm just complaining. But in reality, maybe I'm just trying to place value on what I do each day. Perhaps I'm struggling to feel like I'm doing something worthwhile, and I think that a pay raise will make me feel validated for all of the extra hours I put in. Am I alone in this? I doubt it because it can make you feel very small when you don't feel like a valued member of your community. We can start to question, *What do I get out of this?*

How can we quantify the value of an education provided by a loving teacher who pours their heart into their lesson plans, relationships with students, and classroom environment? How can we put a price tag on the extra time after school spent consoling a miserable student or tutoring a child who is struggling? What is the value of a teacher who cheers for their students at sporting events, music concerts, robotics competitions, or drama productions? What should we earn for the hour-long phone calls reassuring parents and building up caregivers who feel they aren't doing a good job? Honestly, I don't know. Can you truly place a monetary value on the work we do every day? On the extra hours we spend in our classrooms instead of at home with our own families? On the time spent worrying about that kid who we know has zero support at home and needs a champion? I don't know about you, but I don't think so.

So if what we do each day doesn't have a monetary value, what do we get out of this? When I was thinking about this idea the other day, a quote I've heard many times popped into my head. "You get out what you put in." At first, I laughed. I laughed because that has to be one of the quotes that least exemplifies the issue at hand. If teachers got out what they put in, we'd all be millionaires. We'd all be jetting off to our vacation home every summer to bask in the lap of luxury. We wouldn't be buying off-brand school supplies to stock our classroom cupboards, or thrifting for books for our classroom libraries, or skipping out on happy hour with our friends because payday is next Friday. If teachers got out what we put in, I can't think of a single teacher that would go home feeling underappreciated or undervalued. Unfortunately, the writer of that particular quote wasn't thinking about teachers.

Sure, we can go out and take classes for lane changes and pay raises. Yes, we can go out and earn a graduate degree to increase our paychecks. But even then, many teachers feel that they are not getting paid what they ought to based upon the work they do each day.

Let's face it. We as teachers put in WAY more than we will ever get out. More time, more energy, and more of ourselves. But what makes it worth it? What makes us say, "Yes, this is why I'm here." I can't speak for all of us, but I can speak for myself on this matter. It's the kids. I know it's super cliché, but it's true.

Those little weirdos are what get me out of bed in the morning. Those kids are what stop me from applying for that other really cool job I'd probably get if I tried. These goofy, frustrating, endearing, curious, young people make me realize every school year that, yes, it's worth it. It's worth the late-night cry sessions when I tell my husband I can't do this anymore. It's worth the hours spent grading those research papers I curse myself for assigning. It's worth the endless stream of parent emails and student questions and staff meetings and curriculum redesigns and extra hours spent planning lessons my kids will love because I get to see those weirdos' faces every day. I get to push them to reach for their potential. I get to watch the light bulbs go off in their eyes. I get to comfort them when they are freaking out about whatever else is going on in their lives. I get to give them grace when they need it and watch them grow because of it.

On top of it all, I have a front-row seat to their successes. I get to watch them take pride in themselves and their abilities. I get to witness them going from a state of cluelessness to one of mastery. My classroom is home to it all. I don't know about you all, but that seems like pretty good compensation for what I put in. I get to mentor a new group of young people every year. Teachers get to impact the lives of our students every day.

Think back to your teachers. I'll bet you remember the ones who put in more than they needed to. Those teachers noticed you, gave you their time and energy, and they'd probably do it all again if they knew it was helping you. I'll bet they'd even remember you if you saw them today. Now we get to be those teachers. We get to be the ones that make a difference, show up for our students, and help them to grow. We get to guide them through challenging times in their lives and celebrate with them in good times. We get to inspire, to encourage, and to foster our students' passions in life. This, all of this, is what we get out of being a teacher.

So what does this mean for you?

I think we've all seen or at least heard of a lot of self-help books that preach an attitude of gratitude. Now, I know that it can be difficult to do, but if you saw what I wrote about what I get out of teaching and you feel the same, don't we both have something to be grateful for? If we can look at our teaching careers and think, "Yes, this is my calling," I think an attitude of gratitude is called for. Not many people can say they've found their calling. A true vocation, like teaching, is not easy to come by.

Pause for Reflection:

Stop and remember the last challenging student(s) you were able to help. What did you get from that experience?

What aspects of your work as a teacher are your favorites? Which of these things are reasons to feel gratitude?

How can you use that gratitude to help fuel you on challenging days?

When we were little kids, we dreamed big dreams. As for me, I wanted to be an Olympic gymnast. I watched the Magnificent Seven on television, and I thought there was nothing I would ever want more than to be one of them. Then, reality sunk in and I didn't make the competitive gymnastics team. Oh, how I cried when my mom told me the news. But my mom, being the supportive parent she is, pushed me to keep going and find something new to shoot for. So I tried ballet. From that moment on, I was going to be a professional ballerina. Unfortunately for me, that dream, too, was squashed. My instructor told me I would be too short and my legs were too chubby to be a ballerina. Needless to say, I was crushed. She was right, of course. I am too tall to be a gymnast and too short and curvy to be a ballerina. In one year, both of my dreams were dashed.

Both of my parents were teachers at the time, and I loved watching them grade and lesson plan at our dining room table. I looked at them and thought, I could do that. And in the blink of an eye, a new dream was born. I was going to be a teacher, and while my rebellious teenage-self fought against this notion for a few years, here I am, a teacher. And I wouldn't change it. Really, I wouldn't. Sure, there are days when I want to kick it all to the curb, but then I remember how lucky I am that I have found my vocation. Working with young people is what I was made to do, I just know it.

What about you? Do you feel called to this noble vocation of teaching tomorrow's leaders, nurses, electricians, mechanics, and artists? Do you know you were born to inspire the next generation of speakers, musicians, computer programmers, scientists, and great thinkers? Does it just feel right when you see those sparks of creativity, those moments of clarity, and flashes of innovation in your classroom? If so, then you are like me. You've found your calling. I know it's hard, but I challenge you to remember the importance of what you're doing. I want you to try to find something to be grateful for each day. That way, you'll be inspired to come back, day after day, year after year, because those moments of gratitude are what it's all about.

And ultimately, that's what we get out of all of this.

PART FOUR

Our Resilience

"Sometimes what's meant to break you makes you brave."
—Nell Benjamin, lyricist for *Mean Girls (Musical)*

CHAPTER 11

Setting the Stage

There is a young man I met when he was a freshman. This kid loved acting. And when I say he loved it, I mean he wanted nothing more than to find a way to have theatre or film in his life forever. For the next year, he and I studied acting schools and four-year universities that offered strong programs. We weighed the pros and cons of conservatory-style programs and liberal arts schools. We planned out possible futures for him—all of which would allow him to grow as a performer and do what made his soul happy.

I think I enjoyed it just as much as he did. I shared with him my old dream of taking Broadway by storm after college, how I planned to "make it" in acting myself. He wondered why I didn't go for it. And I told him the truth. When I was in college, a very wise theatre professor told us, "You don't have to have a life in theatre to have theatre in your life." As much as a life of performing and theatre work would make my heart happy, I feel like I'm supposed to be a mom WAY more than I'm supposed to be a performer. I didn't want to discourage him, so I told him how I changed my end goal, not because I didn't think the original dream was possible, but because a new dream had presented itself. I told him about how I wanted to be a parent and a teacher and help all of my students achieve their dreams. He told me that he left my room feeling like his dreams were possible. I remember feeling so fortunate to have a student like that in my class because by working with him, I was achieving my dreams.

Unfortunately, his parents didn't share his enthusiasm and didn't offer much in terms of support. He didn't have them to drive him to and from rehearsal, and they rarely came to support his shows; however, he had a theatre family that saw what a gift he had. He could make anyone happy and was the first to be supportive of *his friends. He was such an amazing addition to the theatre program at our school, and it was a joy to watch him in his element.*

I came to one of his shows after I had left that school for another teaching job. He almost broke character on stage when he saw me right in the audience. He went on to give a remarkable performance, and I couldn't have been prouder.

While he was my student, he and I had the opportunity to travel to a state poetry recitation contest where he wowed me. His presence and his confidence, while masking his nervousness, was incredible to behold. I recall his face and the joy on it as I told him how proud I was to have him represent our school.

Flash-forward a few years to when I ran into him while out for my daughter's birthday party—he seemed like he was finding his way in the world. He isn't acting, but he seemed so happy. He told me that he still hopes to have the arts in his future, and I'm so incredibly proud that he hasn't given up on it. Students like him deserve a chance to dream big. Being in on that dream was such a privilege. That year, this student inspired me to keep dreaming and keep teaching.

Bouncing back from teacher burnout may look different for each of us, but it absolutely cannot happen unless we set ourselves up for that success. As you find a way to set the stage for your own success, I want you to keep three things in mind:

1. **Self-Care:**

    In the chapter on self-care, we discussed finding a way to care for ourselves amid the chaos in which we all work. But I think the importance of self-care cannot be overstated. Our lives both in and out of school can stretch us to our limits, physically and mentally, and we need to make taking care of ourselves a priority. I want you to take a few minutes right now to think of a few ways you can practice self-care in the next month. Whatever that looks like for you, make it a priority so that you can continue providing your students with the best education experience you can. I want you to write down the ways you have decided to practice self-care in the next month. Write them down in your Reflection Journal, put them in your planner, on your to-do list, or your electronic calendar. Make sure these things are not cast aside for a new project or task. Remember: we cannot fill another person's cup if ours is empty.

Pause to Reflect:

In the next month, I will practice self-care by...

2. **Priorities**:

In the chapter on priorities, I told you about my own struggles with setting my priorities and not letting everything else take over. This can be a challenge for us all, but I want you to think back to your own priorities list. For me, that list has become rather short. On my list are my family, being a good teacher, and making time for my personal goals and dreams. What does this look like for you? If you are a vision board person, you may find it helpful to put these priorities in the center of that space. After all, these priorities are what should guide you in everything you do. Are you not a vision board/artsy person? No worries! A sticky note on your computer or desk can do the trick as well. The point is, if we have a visual reminder of these priorities every day, we can train ourselves to allow these priorities to guide us in everything we do and each new thing we consider taking on. Before you move on from this idea, jot down your top priorities here or in your Journal.

Pause to Reflect:

My top priorities are:

3. **Defining working "full time"**:

We all know that teachers are notorious for working overtime. We don't get paid overtime (unless we are coaching or advising an activity), but we still do it. We push ourselves to grade one more set of quizzes or set up a stations activity in our classrooms or email one more parent, and while these things are valuable and important, they do tend to pile up, making our days long and stressful.

What I want you to do is think of your definition of a full-time job. Does that consist of 40 hours per week? 50 hours? 60? Whatever your definition is, I want you to consider whether or not that is a reasonable work schedule for you. I know that I would love to work 40 hours a week, but I know that I can't do that and still do my job to my standard. I think I need about 45-50 hours a week, and for me, that's doable. Once you've decided upon a reasonable work schedule for yourself, you need to find ways to keep yourself to that schedule. I find that scheduling my children's activities within an hour of my contract time is a great way to keep myself to that schedule. If they need to be at dance by 4:30, we have to leave school by 4:15, no exceptions. Now, think about how you can find ways to keep yourself to your schedule. Remember to set these limits, as they can help you set the stage for your success.

Pause to Reflect:

I will limit myself to the following hours per week in order to maintain my well-being and make time for the other important parts of my life:

I know that when I think about limiting myself to a full-time schedule, even on my own terms, it can be difficult to hold myself accountable. But then I remember, there will always be one more late assignment to grade, one more tweek I could make the notes for tomorrow, or one more book to shelve. There are always things to do as a teacher, but we need to set reasonable limits and then hold ourselves to them if we want to be successful.

When I was going through this process of setting reasonable limits for myself, I found that keeping myself on a schedule really helped. I know that is a bit obvious, especially after we just discussed this topic, but for a person like me whose mind can jump through 20 different ideas in a few minutes, I need constant reminders. I'm like my first-grader, I thrive on routine. So, I mapped out my typical day and looked for some wiggle room. I asked myself:

Could I wake up earlier to fit in some "me time"? Many of the authors whose books I have read on my journey toward a happier life have suggested this. Many of them wake up more than an hour earlier than their family; however, these authors also have the flexibility to have that hour to themselves, then wake the kids, drive them to school, and then come back home to get themselves ready for the day before work. My contract time doesn't allow for that, plus I'm a total night owl, so I threw out that idea.

Could I take an evening to myself every week? My husband actually suggested this. He golfs and plays softball in the summer, which gives him a few evenings to focus on things that make him happy. I considered this as well, and I'll be honest, a night every week to write or play trivia with a friend or just wander around Target by myself was extremely tempting. But then I thought about how much I would miss that evening family time, so I didn't go for that option either.

Could I find a way to maximize my prep time so I didn't have to bring work home as often? That way, I could write at home after the kids go to bed or just watch Netflix with my husband on the couch. I know we've all read the articles and teacher blogs where these magical teachers can have perfect classrooms, grade everything, and design beautiful curriculum, all in 40 hours a week. Well, I knew that wasn't going to work for me. But I could use this time better. Ultimately, maximizing my prep time was a game-changer. To this day, I am able to limit myself to taking home grading and lesson planning to two evenings a week. Even then, I limit myself to an hour or an hour and a half. That's it. After that, I do something to wind myself down.

These limits I have set for myself, along with the commitment to having productive prep periods have changed the game for me in terms of my resiliency and dedication to returning to teaching year after year. It is still a work-in-progress, like more things in life, but it has changed my mindset, my level of preparedness for work, and my life at home for the better.

Yet another important thing to remember is that while teachers can do so much, we are not superheroes. We are not immune to the need for sleep, nor are there enough hours in the day to do everything alone. This is why it is such a good idea to collaborate with other teachers. Maybe you are, like me, your own department, with no other teachers teaching your classes. Maybe you work in a large district in which you have many other teachers with whom you share a course or two. Either way, there are people out there to help you manage everything. For me, I look to teacher bloggers for inspiration, to Teachers Pay Teachers for assignment ideas, and to mentor teachers for support on the tough days. In addition, I communicate openly with my husband when I need extra support and with my teacher friends who understand the pressures of this job.

Regardless of the availability of other teachers in your school or teacher friends with whom you can vent, you still ought to find a way to share the burdens that come with this job. I know that sounds a little harsh, as I'm sure most of us never really think of our students as burdens, but all of the lesson planning, grading, data collection, admin meetings, and parents to deal with, it can often feel like a huge weight on our shoulders. Find yourself some support! There is no shame in not doing everything alone. Even one or two good supporters can make all the difference in the world for a teacher on the verge of burnout. Just know that asking for help and letting other people pick up the slack every once and a while is ok. Everyone needs a hand sometimes, and knowing when to ask for it can be the difference between burning out and fulfilling your vocation as a teacher.

We need to remember that setting the stage for our personal success is crucial. Teachers often use that line on their students, but it applies to us as well. Just as our students need to build foundational skills, work habits, and methods for dealing with adversity, teachers need to focus on self-care, making our priorities clear, and setting limits on what we do. I challenge you to focus on these things so that you too can set yourself up for success each and every day.

CHAPTER 12

Celebrating Progress

*A*m I the only one who gets WAY too excited by the school supplies section at Target every year? Because I can guarantee that I'm WAY more into it than my children are. School supplies signal a fresh start for me—a new year during which I can hopefully be just a little bit more together than I was last year…

Oh, who am I kidding?? It doesn't matter how many cute planners I buy, how many purple pens I stash in my "no students allowed" cup, or how PERFECT my figurative language bulletin board looks, my desk will still be a complete and utter disaster, I will always have a "smile and pretend it's on the lesson plan" day every now and again, and I will still have times when I wonder why in the world I am still a teacher.

But then, it will get better.

It will get better because a student will tell me how much they loved a book I recommended, or because my principal will drop in at just the right time and see my students really engaged, or because I will witness a random act of kindness outside of my classroom. Regardless of how much of a hot mess I feel like sometimes, it keeps getting better. Those darn kids will do something amazing and I will once again have hope for the future.

I have always wondered where the disconnect between what we teach and what we practice started. Why is it that we can make a student feel like they've conquered the world when they write a complete sentence or turn in a project on time, but when it comes to our own little victories, we just pass them over? I see exceptional teachers gloss over their personal wins all the time. Why do we do it? We teach our students to celebrate the little things and see them as stepping stones towards their goals, but we don't do the same thing for ourselves.

Maybe some of you out there are really good at pausing to savor the moment when something goes well, and if that's you, awesome! But that's not me, and I know it's not many of my colleagues or friends either. We dodge compliments, we are hard on ourselves, and we do the opposite of what we encourage our students to do.

Teachers have hypocritical tendencies, we all know it's true. We talk during professional development sessions after shushing our students an hour before. We text and email and scroll social media during meetings after taking phones away from kids that same morning. But I think the worst of our tendencies is the way we ignore the small victories in our classrooms and beat ourselves up for not being "perfect." We cheer on our students as they work hard and praise them when they accomplish things. But we don't do that for ourselves.

I think many of us do this in the hopes of not getting overconfident or complacent. We want to stay on our toes and work hard all the time, but in doing so, we neglect our own victories and focus on what didn't go well. To avoid burning out and to start feeling like successful teachers, we need to start allowing ourselves to feel good about the work we do.

I don't know about you, but I've read the self-help books full of "treat yourself" messages being thrown around left and right. I've read people discussing extravagant things they do for themselves because they are #WorthIt. Now, I'm not saying you aren't worth extravagant grand gestures, I'm saying that I don't think that's always very practical. When people for whom money is no object go out and buy themselves new cars, spend $1,000 at the salon, or jet off to a beach somewhere, I find myself rolling my eyes a bit. That isn't my reality, nor will it ever be, and knowing what I do about teachers' salaries, I doubt it is yours either.

So how do we do this without either breaking the bank or feeling completely self-indulgent? How can we learn to celebrate the things we do well and reward ourselves for reaching our goals? We simply need to accept progress as a stepping stone towards success.

I want you to take a moment to think about your professional goals. Are you just trying to get by right now? Do you dream of someday becoming a principal? Have you always aspired to teach at the college level? Are you hoping to be a career teacher?

Pause to Reflect:

What are your top professional goals?

Whatever they are, I want you to imagine what you would feel like if you accomplished one of your goals. Now let's break those goals down into some manageable steps. I'll use the goal of becoming a career teacher as an example.

1. Planning: If you want to become a "lifer" teacher, you simply cannot live like a first-year teacher forever. You will not be able to sustain that level of stress for your entire career. To prevent and/or alleviate that stress level, you need to find a rhythm. I would make finding this rhythm a priority in your first few years. It will make things much easier for you down the road.

   For me, that means having a rough plan for each unit and then breaking that down by week. This helps me avoid the last-minute scrambling I did as a first-year teacher. (Yes, it still happens sometimes, but I do my best to avoid it.) Before I leave school on Fridays (and I make sure that is by 4:30), I have a plan for the next week. I have my weekly schedule written out and I have at least gathered, if not photocopied, or pre-loaded my Google Classroom with the next week's materials. I find that by making this a priority each Friday, I can go home and enjoy my weekend with my family and not feel I need to work during that time. Keep in mind that I have only repeated a class once; every other year I have had brand new classes to teach, most with very few resources available to me. That means I have to find or create new materials for nearly every lesson. If I can do you, so can you!

2. Continuing Education: Professional development is an important step towards becoming the teacher you want to be. I know that oftentimes many teachers find the professional development we are required to attend to be dull and/or unhelpful. I have found that when I seek out the professional development myself and choose my own courses or resources, I become more "professionally devel-

oped." Also, you don't have to take a formal course for it to count as professional development. Many of the important lessons I've learned have come from Ted Talks, YouTube, books written by teachers, and teacher blogs. Our ever-growing access to information online can be a gamechanger when you're looking to grow as a teacher, but you aren't interested in any of the classes being offered near you.

3. Grace: Grace, or forgiveness, or acceptance, or whatever other term you'd prefer to use has literally saved my teaching career. Whether I'm giving grace to my students after they "forgot" to do their homework for the umpteenth time, or I'm showing grace to a colleague or administrator when I'm feeling unsupported, it's like this huge weight of stress and frustration is lifted from my shoulders. Grace also works when turned inward. Retraining myself to let go of my little mistakes (and the not too little ones) and move on has been, and will remain, a work in progress for years; however, accepting myself as I am, and not only seeing what makes me inadequate in my own eyes, has made this journey so much more manageable.

    Earlier this year, I had spent hours on a skills-based assessment for my sixth graders after a particularly grueling few class periods. I went into that work session grumpy and stressed. Finally, I got it all ready to go, and it was printed and on my desk for the next day. In the morning I came back to find it riddled with errors. Now, I know I made those mistakes because of the mood I was in when creating the test, but I was so mad at myself. To top it all off, the copier was down, so I couldn't just reprint them. I ended up completely recreating the wheel and turning the test into a Google Forms Quiz in the twenty minutes I had before my first class. Needless to say, I was frustrated and sad, but it all worked out in the end. I took a breath, gave myself a little grace, and started my day with a smile for my students. Plus, apparently, other people like those Google Form Quizzes, because that test ended up being my best seller on Teachers Pay Teachers! If I had given up or beat myself up instead of forging ahead, I probably wouldn't have had a successful day, but because I showed myself some grace, I turned that lemon into lemonade and ended up with a win.

This process of breaking down our goals is a great step on the path towards becoming successful teachers, but that is only part of the equation. Not only do we have to work towards our goals, but we need to also recognize our hard work and progress. I'm not saying you should shout it from the mountaintops, but we need to acknowledge the work we are doing. For some, a moment of reflection will make us feel energized and centered enough to move on to the next thing. Others may want something more tangible. Maybe you pick up takeout on the way home on Fridays if your plans are done and you're ready for next week. Maybe you get a massage at the end of the semester to celebrate submitting your grades. Or maybe, like me, you want to start enforcing a strict "pajamas by 5:00" rule in your house to mark the end of each workweek.

Whatever it looks like, teachers need to acknowledge their own successes and celebrate them, no matter how low-key the celebration is. We need to feel good about the work we are doing if we truly want to keep it up for the next 20 or 30 years. Teachers' self-worth can dictate the quality of the work they do, just like it can for any other profession. If you feel like you are good at your job, or at least that you are making progress towards being good at it, you will be motivated to get even better, or at the very least, to keep moving forward.

Pause for Reflection:

Look back to the goals you wrote down for yourself. What are some manageable and measurable steps you can take this year that will help make those dreams a reality?

Our endgame is a fulfilling career in education. To get there, teachers need to value the progress they make along the way, just as we applaud the progress made by our students. The time has come to set aside our hypocritical tendencies and embrace our own success. Without this, how can we possibly achieve our long term goals? I don't want a single one of you to simply exist as a teacher for your whole career. I want you to thrive. I want you to approach this path with joy, and never doubt for a second that you are a good teacher, that you are made for this, and that your students are darn lucky to have you as a teacher.

You have the potential to do so much good in the lives of so many. I have always felt that teachers have one of the coolest jobs in the world, because who else gets to inspire and educate and grow alongside as many people as teachers? We have the power to motivate so many young people to dream big and work hard to get what they want. Now, it is time for you to motivate yourself. Pretend you are a student in your class. What would you say to yourself?

Pause for Reflection:

If I were a student in my own class, the message I would want to hear is...

I know what I needed to hear as a student, so now I'll say it to you:

Don't give up, ever. Don't lose hope, ever. Keep dreaming, always. Ditch the self-doubt. You can do this because you are strong and worthy of a good life.

Teachers, I know this job isn't easy, and I know I've probably said it a dozen times throughout this book, but it's true. It's not easy, and yet here you are. Here you are continuing to work and grow to be the best version of yourself. Here you are planning for and dreaming of, the future. You can do this. You can conquer the self-doubt and embrace your successes. I know you can.

Don't give up. Find value in your progress towards your goals. Dream big, but go easy on yourself when things don't go according to plan. Being perfect isn't possible, we're human after all, so don't expect that of yourself. Give yourself time to plan, space to grow, and the grace you need to feel confident and motivated. If you can do those things, then you can look forward to a happy and successful career as a teacher.

CHAPTER 13

Things Outside of Our Control

A few years ago, I had a student who puzzled me. I can normally read my students pretty well, but this girl was a mystery to me. On one hand, she was really open about parts of her life, but one the other, she was super mysterious about other aspects. I made it my mission to get to the bottom of it because I could feel it in my gut that something was wrong.

This student continued to come to school looking more and more disheveled, and her lack of personal hygiene became an issue in the tight quarters in my classroom. She would fall asleep in the front row and never had her materials with her. Then, her glasses mysteriously disappeared. I finally got her to talk to me about it. She and her family were being evicted from their apartment, and they didn't have any of their belongings, other than what she had in her bag. She had no shampoo, no deodorant, and no toothbrush. When I asked her why she didn't say anything before, she said she was just too embarrassed.

Right away, I'm ashamed to admit, I made a snap judgment about her mom. I thought, "What is her mom doing? I just saw her and she had her nails done and reeked of smoke. Her daughter's basic needs aren't even being met!" Now, I'm sure we've all jumped to making judgments like before. We'll hear a parent say they can't afford a pair of glasses for their child when they have the latest smartphone and smoke a pack a day, or a student's lunch account will be empty for a week, but their parents go on a vacation. It's so hard not to, I know, because we're not perfect, we're human. But this young lady really tugged on my heartstrings, so I got a bit more judgy than I'm proud to admit.

My team and I got her connected with her counselor, and she got to go "shopping" in our school food and personal item closet. She came to school the next day with clean, wet hair and a smile on her face. She was back. As soon as she was equipped to take care of herself, she was back to being herself again. She smiled, she started turning in her homework, and seemed comfortable in her own skin. Before she got the help she needed, many of her basic needs weren't being met. She was too busy dealing with the stress of finding a new place to live and being embarrassed for her appearance to have the energy to devote to school.

Granted, this young lady's stress load is not the norm for sixth graders. Most young people have what they need to get by, and if they don't, we have programs to help them. It can be so tough when they won't tell us about it, but it's even harder when we realize we can help them in the short-term, but everything else is outside our control. I've often had students who I wished I could just bring home with me so I could take care of them, but we can't. We are limited to what we can do in our classrooms and in our schools, and we can only do so much. Things outside of our control like this can be one of the most challenging things about our jobs. We can't control their homes, their parents, or their choices once they leave us, and we have to learn to accept that.

While it's not easy, I like to think about all of the good things I'm able to do for my students each day. I give them a safe place in which I attempt to meet their needs as people and as learners. If they're hungry, I feed them. If they're sad, I comfort them. If they're excited, I celebrate alongside them. If they feel like life outside of school is too much, I connect them with people better equipped to help. At the end of the day, I am doing everything I can for my students, and I will continue to as long as I'm around. While it's not a magic fix, it's how I've learned to cope with these things outside of my control at school.

You may have noticed that other than a few casual mentions, I have steered clear of two big issues that plague many new and veteran teachers alike: student behaviors and a lack of administrative support. While these are extremely valid issues, I don't think this book is the place to go on and on about these issues, as they are things that are out of our control. My aim for this book is for my readers to focus on the things they can change, and unfortunately, we cannot wave a magic wand and end up with perfectly behaved students or our dream version of an administrator. With these things in mind, I would be remiss to gloss over these issues entirely. For many teachers facing burnout, student behaviors and issues with administrators are at the heart of the problem.

If someone had asked me what my top three reasons for considering leaving teaching were, student behaviors would definitely be on the list. Nothing can derail a well-planned lesson like a student acting out and "ruining it" for everyone else. These kids can be a challenge, to say the least. But as we all know, these kids aren't evil. Some of them have had evil things done to them, or in their presence, that have left scars that will last forever. These are the kids who need us to love them even more.

In Chapter 3, I quoted a former principal by saying, "Every kid needs an adult who's crazy about them." We all know this to be true. Every young person needs someone who is in their corner, but I know how hard that is. It can be extremely challenging to wrap a kid up in love after they have yelled obscenities at you. It can be tough to root for the naughty kid after they torment their peers for weeks on end. If you are thinking it's impossible, then you aren't alone. I used to feel that way, and I know some of my colleagues still do too. But despite all of those things, we have to do it. If we don't, who will?

Our students need us, especially the challenging ones. At some point, an adult is going to make a huge impression on them, for better or for worse. Wouldn't it be great if we could set these kids up for success and support them from the moment they walk through our doors? That way, they at least know there is an adult somewhere who has their back. It just takes a lot of grace on our parts.

I wrote earlier about grace and how it has been a game-changer for me. Grace and understanding can go a long way with challenging students. For some of them, they are used to fast reactions to their behaviors, often yelling or other violent responses. They are conditioned to that, so the little things such as sitting in the corner, or going to the principal just aren't a big deal to them. Sure, it gets them out of sight and out of mind for a bit, but it doesn't actually fix anything. In fact, some of them want to be removed from class or are seeking this attention in negative ways, so sending them away is more of a reward than a punishment. We cannot alter students' behaviors, but we can influence them.

Think about the adults who influenced you the most. I'll bet that for most of us, a teacher is on that list. I had a teacher who handled student discipline in a way that should have won him a gold medal. One day, he had to remove a student from my class because he was so far out of line, none of us could get anything done. He tried all of the usual tactics, but this kid was there to intentionally cause issues that day. My teacher never raised his voice, he never belittled the student, and he didn't bad-mouth him or show that anything had happened once he had left the room.

The next day, that student walked back into class, a bit sheepishly, and was met by our teacher. The teacher walked up to him, shook his hand, and said, "Let's have a good day." That was it. No shame, no guilt trip, and no grudge. My classmate just went to his desk, took a few moments to let it sink in, and then rejoined our class as if nothing had happened. From that point on, he never acted up in that class again. It was amazing. Even as a student, I knew I had witnessed something really cool. I aspire to be like my teacher was, and still is. He treated us with dignity, even when we messed up. He never took it personally or held a grudge. Everyone got a fresh start every day.

The next time a student acts out in your classroom, I want you to remember that we all have stuff we deal with outside of school, and young people, like our students, often don't have many of the tools needed to deal with those issues. Over the years, teachers have accumulated many tools in our emotional toolboxes after dealing with parents, administrators, and students who have pushed our buttons, along with everything that has happened in our personal lives. Remember that our students' toolboxes are still pretty empty. I don't know about you, but I didn't learn the tools for dealing with the most difficult emotions until I was much older, and I had a ton of support along the way. Oftentimes, our challenging students are working with empty emotional toolboxes and have zero support outside of school. As hard as it is, remember that their choices are not in your control; you can only control how you react to them.

Another thing outside of our control is our administrators. Now I have been fortunate enough at times to work for some of the best administrators I've ever met; however, that also means I haven't always been so lucky. I'm sure most of you are with me there. Your relationship with your administrator can make or break many parts of this job. If you get along with your administrator, it can feel like discipline and academic issues are handled gracefully, but if you don't see eye-to-eye, it can feel like they are playing favorites elsewhere.

So how do we deal with administrators with whom we don't work well? Unfortunately, there is no perfect solution. Every administrator is so different and you can get vastly different levels of support depending on the situation, just as teachers are going to react to things differently depending on what is happening. I know that some days the little things don't bug me, but on other days, it's hard not to snap at my students. We all deal with those inconsistencies within our own hearts and minds, but for some reason, we feel like the principal shouldn't get to be inconsistent. We put administrators on this pedestal upon which they are not allowed to waver.

Now I realize that a principal's job looks very different than ours. They're the ones who have to step in after everything we've tried doesn't work. Oftentimes, I'm sure they miss the classroom because so many of their inter-actions with students are because the student made a poor choice. Where we may have to deal with one or two naughty kids a day, they may have to work with a dozen or more. In fact, I'm so glad there are people out there who want to be principals because frankly, I don't think I could do it. My dad was a principal and a darn good one. He has such a calming and steady presence and has this way of calming everyone else down too. I can speak from experience from when I was an angsty and emotional teenager, he's the best. But I'm sure even he had his days.

What I am saying is, our principals are outside of our control, and they are human too. Unless you want the job yourself, teachers need to let go of our preconceived notions of what a principal should or should not be. Their job, like ours, is challenging. Yes, they make more money than we do, which can be a hard pill to swallow, but they face challenges that we don't have to deal with. I've always felt that the best administrators let teachers do what we do best: teach. Perhaps we can return the favor. Of course, make your voice heard if something is wrong, but otherwise, the actions of our administrators are simply not in our control.

Hopefully, your administrator is a good leader whose actions are guided by what's best for students. That's what I always hope for. Unfortunately for us, what's best for kids isn't always what is best or most convenient for teachers. This can be really challenging. If your administrator asks you to completely revamp your curriculum, or allow time in your classes for counseling lessons, or to switch grades or classes entirely, that can be tough. But at the end of the day, we are here for the kids, right? We are guided by what's best for kids, and hopefully so are our administrators, so being on the same team can make this job a much easier thing to take on.

Things outside of our control are just that, out of our control. Yes, diffi-cult students and administrators can make this job much harder than it would be otherwise, but we can't let that stop us. We cannot allow a few people to derail what can be a fulfilling career in education. Maybe a difficult adminis-trator will inspire you to pursue an administrative role yourself, or maybe it'll solidify that your place is in the classroom.

Either way, I encourage you to look beyond these things that are outside of our control and focus on what we can change: our attitudes, our work habits, and the way we react to difficult situations. If we get those things working smoothly, it becomes easier to let that rude student's comments roll right off of you; it becomes easier to take negative feedback from an administrator with an open mind; it becomes easier to become and remain a resilient teacher.

Pause for Reflection:

Think about the aspects of our job that are out of your control. How can you learn to let go of these things and focus upon the aspects that you can control?

CHAPTER 14

Gratitude and Growth Mindsets

One of my favorite stories about a random act of kindness happened in a hallway outside of the gym. Picture this: two varsity football players are sauntering down the hall to class, jerseys on, ready to play a big game that night. A female student with special needs is crying in the hallway. Now, these boys could have kept walking, and no one would have blamed them. But they didn't. One of the boys (who happened to be super popular: he was an athlete, on the Homecoming Court, and generally a very well-liked young man) stopped and handed his books to his friend. I froze in my tracks and watched this scene play out. I thought to myself, he'd better not mess with her. Shame on me for ever doubting him. This young man handled this situation with such kindness and class that I just looked on in awe. He asked his friend to tell the teacher he'd be late and started to walk towards the crying girl. He greeted her by name, put his arm around her, and in the gentlest way, asked her what was wrong.

It turns out that she was late for class. Being late and the fear of disappointing others were especially tough for this girl. Instead of just going to class himself, this young man comforted her, and then walked her to class, telling her everything would be all right. I couldn't take my eyes off it for one second. It was a moment when if I had had her number, I would have called that boy's mom and told her what a classy young man he was. Instead, I went back to my classroom, my heart feeling lighter than it had all day. It is moments like that that make me grateful to be a teacher and inspire me to keep going because these young people can be absolutely remarkable.

When I was growing up, teaching and education were frequent topics of conversation at the dinner table, especially during the holidays. Not only are my parents educators, but so are my aunt and uncle. Plus, I have another aunt who worked as a registrar at a high school. My youngest brother is also a teacher, making for a group of people who are, understandably, focused on educational issues. We swap stories, my brother and I swap lesson ideas, and we discuss big picture issues like national standards and testing. I almost feel bad for the non-teachers in the room…almost.

It's so cool to hear my family members so passionately speak about what really matters to them, the students. At the end of the day, that's really what matters. I could read it so clearly, even in my younger years, that teaching was not just a job for these people, it was their calling, their vocation. I remember wanting that sense of purpose for myself someday. I didn't know if it would be as a teacher, but I knew that passion and commitment to what really matters would need to be present for me to feel fully fulfilled in my job. Luckily for me, I didn't have to look too far for that calling.

Deciding to be a teacher was not a quick decision for me. Before settling into my education program, I belonged to what my family called the "major of the month club." I was indecisive and worried that I would make the wrong choice. I didn't want to pigeon-hole myself into one career path with no alternatives. There were so many things I could see myself doing with my life. I had been a theatre kid in high school and considered a conservatory program in vocal performance so I could open up a voice studio in my home someday. Since I loved school, I contemplated completing my English degree and going to graduate school, with the hope of teaching at college or university someday. I am an advocate for those whose voices are often overlooked, so I considered law school. I love books and history, and so I got an internship in a university archive. All of these choices mulled around in my head and heart throughout my college years.

Then, it hit me. Where could I combine all of my passions? In a school, of course. I could get involved with the theatre department and share my love of performance and music. I could continue to geek out over books and literary analysis in my classroom. I could amass a classroom library full of classics and new volumes to appeal to the many types of readers in my school. I could teach and learn history alongside my students. My mind was made up. I declared an English Education major and now I get to teach a little bit of every one of my passions. Do I sometimes worry that I am not cut out for this? You bet I do, but I know that I made the right choice for me. Teaching was always in my blood, I just needed to realize it.

I know I've mentioned it before, but the notion of a vocation is something to which I have always aspired. I believe there is great value in not only finding one's vocation but also in earning a living doing it. So how can we learn to find this value in what we do? How can we shift our mindset from one that is exhausted and feeling overworked to one full of gratitude for the amazing calling that we embraced since we became teachers?

Just like any mindset shift, this takes a leap of faith on our parts. I know we've all seen and heard the stories of people who are taking charge of their lives and embracing a mindset of gratitude, and frankly, a lot of that sounds super cheesy to me. I know that sounds harsh. Those people are doing wonderful things for so many people, but they aren't teachers. I don't know about you, but I don't think I can make time for the meditation sessions and journaling and everything else I see promoted online. Do those things work? I'm sure they do, but they don't work in my life. I needed something different.

What I've found works for me is a practice my parents taught me from a young age. Every night, we all said a prayer of gratitude for all of the wonderful people in our lives. Now, I'm not asking you to do that. I know that not everyone's spiritual and/or religious lives look like mine, but the act of taking a moment at the end of each day to be grateful for the good things is something I do to this day. Each night, I close my eyes and replay the day. I think about the good things and the bad. I take a moment to be grateful for the good things that happened and to reflect upon the bad. I go to bed with an outlook that sets myself up for a good day when I wake up in the morning. It looks something like this (here's an example from my day yesterday):

- What went well today?
  - My daughter's enthusiasm for reading was infectious! I picked up a book right along with her.
  - I got to share my love of Harry Potter with my children.
  - My husband and I had a good workout.
  - I made my Grandma's apple crisp recipe— yum!

- What didn't go well today?
  - I snapped at my children for making a mess right after I cleaned.

- I wasn't as present as I could have been. I spent too much time on my computer.
- I was reluctant to leave the house again.

- What can I do to make tomorrow better?
  - Remember that I need to let my kids be kids. We can always clean up later.
  - Maybe we should do a project together tomorrow? Painting? Baking?
  - I will go on a walk with the kids and maybe do some work in the yard.

This process sounds really simplistic and may seem a bit cheesy to some of you, but ending the day with this reflection is so helpful for me. I get to remember the good things and focus my energy on what I can do better next time. Plus, I don't need a fancy journal or a meditation track to do it. I can simply spend a few minutes each day focused upon gratitude and self-reflection.

Now, I challenge you to try it. I want you to reflect upon the last 24 hours and focus on it with a positive mindset.

Pause to Reflect:

What went well today?

What didn't go well today?

What can I do to make tomorrow better?

When we can go from a negative mindset to a growth mindset (yes, like the one we push upon our students), we can start to see positivity and room for growth in everything we do. This growth mindset can be the difference between giving up on this career and powering through a difficult school year. It can be the difference between throwing in the towel after a difficult encounter with an administrator and taking their feedback in stride.

We all have room to grow, and teaching is the perfect catalyst for that growth. We get to learn right alongside our students, we get to try and fail, and we get to get better every year. Very few first-year teachers go down in history as the best teachers of all time. We all need time to grow into the teachers we will become.

Earlier I mentioned a lesson I learned from a wise administrator in which he reminded us that we are planting trees, not wheat. Now, he was referring to our students, but I would apply that same metaphor to teachers. While our school years are fleeting, our careers are the opposite. Our careers in education are long-lasting and ever-growing. Our root systems are the years we spend in classrooms wherever we go. Our branches are the things we learn and the ways we grow as educators. And our leaves are the many students we have the opportunity to teach throughout our careers.

So yes, it is important to work towards our goals to continue to improve our craft. But there's no rush towards perfection. There's no pressure to change the world in a single school year. I can't think of a single person who could do that in such a short time. Besides, changing the world isn't even the goal. The goal is to change the lives of the students we teach. Teachers can do this in little snapshots of excellence in our lessons or our interactions with our students, which can be educational or even relational. Bottom line: we don't need to be superheroes. We just need to be willing to grow.

When we stop to think about all of this, we can see that a growth mindset is key to achieving success as a teacher. We must not only be willing to develop our talents and skills over our careers but also to acknowledge the fact that even within and among all of the crazy stressors we deal with daily, in school and at home, we have things for which we ought to be grateful. We ought to be grateful for our students, even when they make us want to pull our hair out. We ought to be grateful for the opportunity to inspire the next generation of young adults who will go forth and do amazing things. We ought to be grateful for the fact that a student somewhere credits us for inspiring them to keep going when things get tough.

Gratitude and growth are tough, and I fully recognize that. It's taken almost completely burning out from the stress of this job and everything that comes with it for me to realize all of this. It is hard to feel grateful when someone has yelled obscenities at you in front of a room of students. It's tough to feel grateful when it feels like no one listens to you. It's hard to find gratitude when all of your hard work on a big project seems to fall apart because a student says it's stupid or boring.

It's tough, and I won't deny it, but think about the good you are doing every day. You are teaching students more than standards, more than class content. You are teaching perseverance, diligence, self-confidence, and so much more. You are helping young people recognize and strive towards their potential. Teachers do so much more than people think. I challenge you to find joy in the little things, value progress, but most importantly, I urge you to continue to grow as a teacher. There is no limit to what you can do with this amazing vocation you have chosen.

Despite all of this, teachers still burn out. They burn out even with all of the success they experience in their classrooms. People leave our profession because it's really hard to be a teacher, and I get it, I really do. If you are feeling that way right now, please take heart because we are all right there with you. We are all tired. We are all stressed. You are not failing if you are feeling these things. Pause to remember all of the good you do for your students every day, and don't let go of that gratitude. Use it to fuel you on the days when it feels like you are undervalued or underappreciated.

Remember: you are not alone in what you are feeling. Teaching can be a very thankless job, but there is a reason we all chose it. Most of those reasons are as unique as each of us are, but I'll bet we have one reason in common. We are here for those students we have the privilege to teach year after year—yes, even the challenging ones. We are here for their success stories, lightbulb moments, sparks of potential, and personal victories.

We are here to be the catalyst that motivates young people to be their best. We are here to inspire students to succeed, against whatever odds are stacked against them. We are here to be their teachers. In the end, that's what it all comes down to: we are teachers, and our resilience is what will fuel the next generation of learners.

ACKNOWLEDGMENTS

*T*his book is the compilation of many of the lessons I have learned in my first seven years of teaching, and it has been a joy to write. But it never would have happened without the help of some very important people in my life.

My husband, Lucas, has been my rock throughout this entire process. Thank you for pushing me to complete this project, even when I was losing steam. Your encouragement has been just what I needed to fulfill this dream of mine. Thank you for the late-night nachos and wine and your calming presence as I brought this book out of my head and onto the page. Thank you for believing in me when I didn't believe in myself. I couldn't ask for a better partner.

My daughters, Nora and Alice, inspire me daily to reach for my dreams. Thanks, girls, for helping Mommy write this book. I don't think I could have finished the ending without you doing yoga in the background, bringing me pictures to decorate my desk, or giving me random snuggles on my big writing days. You are such lights in my life. I'm a lucky Mommy.

My parents raised me in a home full of learning. They encouraged me to follow in their footsteps and become a teacher. Thanks, Mom and Dad, for being the best teachers I ever had.

My students are a constant source of inspiration. To my students, past and present, I'm so proud to be your teacher. It is a privilege to learn alongside you and to encourage you to dig deep and never give up. I sincerely cannot wait to see what an amazing influence you will be on our world.

Finally, thank YOU. Yes, you, the teacher who took a chance on my book. If you are feeling burnt out or lost, please remember that you are not alone. You are stronger than you know, for this calling is not for the faint of heart.

I WELCOME YOUR FEEDBACK!

As a reflective practitioner, I am continually looking for ways to improve my craft, both in the classroom and in the resources I produce for other teachers.

I hope you have found value in this resource, but either way, I would appreciate it if you would leave me an honest review to help me as I write and create new resources for teachers like you and me.

Thank you!

—Jaclyn Reuter